S0-AGK-382

ANTONIO PAOLUCCI

Michelangelo and Raphael in the Vatican

EDIZIONI MUSEI VATICANI

G GIUNTI   sillabe

cover:
Michelangelo
The Creation of Adam (1508-1512)
Sistine Chapel, the Ceiling

Raphael
The School of Athens (1509)
Room of the Segnatura

ISBN 978-88-8271-307-2

© 2013 Edizioni Musei Vaticani
Vatican City
www.museivaticani.va

Editorial Direction
Antonio Paolucci, Arnold Nesselrath, Paolo Nicolini

Texts
Antonio Paolucci

Editorial Coordination
Federico Di Cesare

Editors
Carla Cecilia (general supervisor)
Valerio Brienza, Cristina D'Andrea, Simona Tarantino

Photo Credits
Foto © Musei Vaticani
Images selected by: Rosanna Di Pinto, Filippo Petrignani
Photographs by: Pietro Zigrossi and Alessandro Bracchetti,
Giampaolo Capone, Luigi Giordano, Danilo Pivato,
Alessandro Prinzivalle
Unless otherwise specified in the photo credits,
copyright of the images published in this book
is property of the Vatican Museums.

By courtesy of the Amministrazione del Patrimonio
della Sede Apostolica: p. 140
By courtesy of the Fabbrica di San Pietro in Vaticano:
pp. 8, 11-13, 138, 141-143
By courtesy of the Fondazione Casa Buonarroti: p. 53
By courtesy of the Ministero dei beni
e delle attività culturali e del turismo: p. 7

*All rights reserved. Translation, electronic memorisation,
reproduction, full or partial adaptation by any means
(including microfilm and photocopying) are strictly
prohibited in all countries.*

First edition: December 2013

Printed by Tipografia Vaticana

Reprint	Year
5 4 3 2 1 0	2016 2015 2014 2013

Published by:
Giunti Editore S.p.A.
Via Bolognese 165 - 50139 Florence - Italy
Via Borgogna 5 - 20122 Milan - Italy
www.giunti.it

s i l l a b e s.r.l.
Scali d'Azeglio 22 - 57123 Livorno - Italy
www.sillabe.it - info@sillabe.it

Editorial Management
Claudio Pescio,
Maddalena Paola Winspeare

Editor
Augusta Tosone

English Translation
Julia Hanna Weiss

Graphic design, cover and layout
Grafica Punto Print srl, Rome

Image coordination
Nicola Dini

Contents

Michelangelo
in the Vatican

The *Pietà* in Saint Peter's Basilica

Michelangelo
Pietà (1499)

Vatican City, Saint Peter's Basilica

The Virgin Mary, with the features of a young girl, holds and contemplates the body of her Son taken down from the cross. The sculpture conveys a feeling of deep calm, filled with grief and drama.

at the beginning of the chapter:

Jacopino del Conte
Portrait of Michelangelo (c. 1550-1560)

Florence, Casa Buonarroti

The first, instantaneously clear impression we get when looking at the *Pietà* in Saint Peter's Basilica that Michelangelo signed in 1499 when he was only twenty-four years old, is identical to what Giorgio Vasari wrote in the first edition of the *Lives* (1550). "It is certainly a miracle that a stone without any shape at the beginning should ever have been reduced to such perfection as Nature is scarcely able to create in the flesh"[1].

The astonishment Giorgio Vasari expressed is exactly the same that the thousands of tourists who walk by the statue daily feel today. For us, as for Vasari, the *Pietà* is a miracle, a miracle of supreme skill.

The statue stands before us like a jewel: pure, polished and gleaming. We admire the splendour of the flesh, the marvel of the draperies rendered with infinite skill and, like the author of the *Lives*, we think that it is unsurpassable in the art of sculpture. Along with Vasari, we are forced to acknowledge that if art and skill are the metamorphosis that transforms a stone into an imitation of life and into a visible image of an idea, this statue is a miracle in the true sense of the word, that is to say, no such perfection had ever been achieved before.

I believe that the first person to be convinced that he had achieved the incomparable, at least in terms of formal perfection, was Michelangelo himself, and that is why he decided to sign the *Pietà*. According to Vasari, he wanted to sign it because he was satisfied and proud of it. But this comment only appears in the first edition of the *Lives*. In the second edition (1568), he replaced it with a rather banal and unconvincing statement which explains the signature as the desire to authenticate the authorship of a sculpture that someone would have attributed to another. I prefer the first version. They are words that match the pride and awareness of a youthful miracle. That signature could indeed gratify the twenty-four year old Michelangelo's confident immaturity.

If the true meaning of the Saint Peter's *Pietà* is its intact perfection (a superb and luminous finish of the skins which is not "an extra" but a way of expressing both the intellectual and spiritual concept), then we can understand why the world considered the 1972 act of vandalism, perpetrated by a psychopath who took a hammer to the tip of the Virgin's nose and left eye, a true devastation. We can also understand why the restorations (for once violating all the hallowed principles) aimed at, and succeeded in, perfectly repairing the violated face.

Existing casts made it possible to restore the damaged parts of the Virgin's face with total approximation. In this way, the trauma of 1972 did not diminish "the smooth and silvery pallor of that unforgettable face" (Brandi 1994).

No matter how distressing, similar visible damage would have been tolerated on any other statue. But not on the Vatican *Pietà* because the formal perfection – the "miracle" Giorgio Vasari so admired – is the distinctive feature of this sculpture, it is the main reason that makes it so fascinating.

The Virgin's face is that of a very young woman, almost a child, and certainly much younger than the man she holds on her knees, the man who is her Son. To those who pointed out this incongruity (how could Christ seem older than His Mother?), Michelangelo replied – and again, this is Vasari's version – that Youth is the mirror and embodiment of Virginity and in giving Mary the image of an adolescent girl, he wanted to emphasize the uncontaminated purity of the Mother of God.

The theological explanation of this unusual iconography (in Western religious art, Mary at the foot of the Cross, or contemplating the dead Christ, is always depicted as an older woman) is totally convincing. In addition, she is the transposition into a visible image of Dante's famous lines that Michelangelo knew so well: "Virgin Mother, daughter of thine own Son, humble and exalted more than any other creature" (*Paradise* XXXIII, 1-2)[2].

This is to say that there is a sublime religious reflexion in the Virgin's face. It is a face that must be real: the image of a supremely beautiful girl whom no one had ever seen before and yet that we would recognize if we were to come across her. It is a face that must seem eternal because the Madonna is a timeless icon, and the embodiment of the Church that is alive and holy by virtue of the Body of Christ. It is a face that must symbolize the grief of all the mothers in the world through the pensive sorrow of a child-mother whose Son was conceived by the Holy Spirit. The face of the Virgin in the Vatican *Pietà* is, therefore, an example of spiritual beauty. This mimesis of Truth (a Truth that idealizes and transfigures Nature) becomes the vehicle of profound theological meanings: the Immaculate Conception, the Word that becomes flesh, the mystery of the death of God, Mary-Church witness and guardian of the *Corpus Domini*.

In the Virgin's face we see in full the concept of "spiritual beauty" that Michelangelo pursued. Viewed from the front, Mary appears serious and thoughtful; her youth seems timeless, and yet, it is as old as the world. Seen in profile, the Virgin reveals the awkward shyness of a child called to contemplate a mystery that is greater than she.

It is only in the frescoes by Beato Angelico in San Marco, Florence (frescoes that Michelangelo certainly saw and admired) that we find portrayals of the Virgin Mary which are so profoundly spiritual and at the same time so real, real in the sense of a moving simplicity that is comprehensible to all.

It is certainly no accident that the Vatican *Pietà,* like the *Annunciation* by Beato Angelico, has come down through the centuries as a basic image of popular devotion that is widely beloved even today.

At this point, we have to ask where the Vatican *Pietà,* this miracle of "ability" and "grace" (to use the words of the early authors), fits into Michelangelo's career? In which cultural and stylistic world did the *Pietà* take shape? What are the precedents that explain it? These are not easy questions because, at the first impact, the statue in Saint Peter's in the Vatican seems like a glowing meteorite that fell to earth from another world. Its formal perfection, and the effect of something never seen before, as described by Vasari, are so great that we are tempted to say that the only explanation for the *Pietà* is the *Pietà* itself.

It is an understandable suggestion, but it is also dangerous and we have to be wary, because no one is, or can be, removed from history, not even Michelangelo. Therefore, we have to place the *Pietà* in its own era and try to understand the historical reasons that led to this outcome.

The patron who commissioned the statue was the Frenchman Jean Bilhères de Lagraulas cardinal of the titular

Michelangelo
Pietà (1498-1499)
The Virgin's face damaged by the act of vandalism (left)
and after the 1972 restoration (right).

church of Santa Sabina, better known to his contemporaries as the Cardinal of Saint-Denis. It is well-known that he was rich, powerful, and the French ambassador to the papal court. That he was an educated man is evident from his friendship with Jacopo Galli, the Florentine banker and collector who owned the *Bacchus* (now in the Museo Nazionale del Bargello, in Florence) that Michelangelo had carved for Cardinal Raffaele Riario between 1496 and 1497.

It is also significant that it was Jacopo Galli who guaranteed for the contract for the Saint Peter's *Pietà* which was signed on 27 August 1498, and that he committed himself on behalf of Michelangelo with words that went well beyond the customary legal phrases.

The twenty-three year old Buonarroti delivered the finished sculpture within a year. Anticipating what would be Giorgio Vasari's opinion fifty years later, Galli, the banker, wrote "it will be the most beautiful marble piece we have in Rome today, and that no other master could surpass today.

In any event, whether the Cardinal of Saint-Denis was familiar with Michelangelo's statues in Rome, as is most likely, or whether he trusted Galli's guarantees, what is certain is that the statue was meant for the Chapel of Saint Petronilla (where the cardinal is buried) – the Chapel of the King of

France in the old Saint Peter's basilica, and therefore he dedicated his utmost attention to the project. From archive documents we know that he personally and repeatedly pressured the Anziani of Lucca and the Signoria of Florence to "provide marble and helpers for Michele Agnolo di Ludovico statuary". It is likely that the patron himself requested the iconography of the "Grieving Mother" with the body of her Son on her lap since it was a very popular image beyond the Alps and was particularly venerated in France. This sculpture seemed even more appropriate since the chapel of Saint Petronilla was the French national chapel and the Cardinal of Saint-Denis, ambassador of the king of France, was well aware that had to represent his country's culture and traditions in Rome. It is also possible that memories of Italian models from Lombardy and Emilia, such as the *Pietà* by Ercole de' Roberti (now in Liverpool), which Michelangelo had certainly seen and admired when he was working in Bologna, influenced the sculpture.

However, there was no lack of iconographic models to inspire him in Florence. Of the many, we must at least mention the *Pietà* that Perugino painted for San Giusto degli Ingesuati around 1494 and is now in the Uffizi.

In any book on the history of art, the Saint Peter's *Pietà* could legitimately and effectively be the last image at the end of the chapter devoted to fifteenth century sculpture. And this is not so much because it is dated 1499, but because it seems to be (and in fact is) the apex, the supreme fruit of the artistic culture of spirituality and the "styles" of the fifteenth century.

We mentioned the iconography, that was typical of the fifteenth century and widespread in the north, but also in the Po Valley and Florentine area. For reasons of simplicity we mentioned Ercole de' Roberti and Perugino. We could add the names of the great Donatello, the young Buonarroti's guiding star as we see in the *Madonna of the Stairs* (c. 1490) in Casa Buonarroti, as well as Luca della Robbia for the pure splendour of his white majolica sculp-

tures and, as noted by Frederick Hartt (1975), Antonio Rossellino when he carved the Tomb of the Cardinal of Portugal in San Miniato in Florence.

As to the world of ideas and religious sensitivities we could dwell at length on Neo-Platonism, the currency of the intellectuals and artists of the day, and even longer on "Savonarolism".

We should not forget that while the *Pietà* was taking shape, the fire that eliminated the prophetic monk who was executed in Piazza della Signoria in Florence in May 1498 was still burning in the Christian conscience of Florentines and certainly of Michelangelo. He was a deeply religious man and was certainly influenced by the Savonarolian aesthetic which held that "exterior beauty" cannot exist if it does not emerge from the "beauty of the soul".

In brief, behind the young Michelangelo there was the archaizing and Neo-Platonic culture of the Giardino di San

Marco where he studied under the protection of Lorenzo the Magnificent between 1489 and 1492. There was also the nearby Dominican monastery of San Marco, that was the stronghold of Savonarolian spirituality.

All this is to say that Michelangelo's early works had their roots in the fifteenth century. And so did the *Pietà*.

In any event, all the memories and suggestions I mentioned became something new in the Vatican *Pietà*. Just as the *Bacchus* in the Bargello is both Michelangelo's most ancient-style statue and the first sixteenth century nude, the *Pietà* is both totally fifteenth century and totally new. The evocation was transformed into a glorious and astounding beginning. It may be that Michelangelo presented the cultural world behind the *Pietà* (competition with Antiquity, the awareness of the great fifteenth century artistic tradition) with a certain amount of self-satisfaction, a

sort of youthful arrogance. However, any earlier male nude (by Pollaiolo, Verrocchio, Botticelli) will seem fatally antiquated when compared with the anatomy of this dead Christ. The Vatican *Pietà* ended one century and began another that would be entirely (and this statue proves it with amazing clarity) dominated by Michelangelo.

Michelangelo
Pietà (1498-1499)
Detail of Christ's face.

Pietà
Detail of Michelangelo's signature on the diagonal band.

Pietà
Detail of the Virgin's face.

The Sistine Chapel

The Fifteenth Century Frescoes, before Michelangelo

If the *Pietà* in Saint Peter's Basilica is his youthful masterpiece, the murals in the Sistine Chapel, slightly less than two thousand square meters of fresco populated with hundreds of figures, traverse Michelangelo's prime and the latter part of his career. Michelangelo painted the ceiling between 1508 and 1512 when he was a young man, between thirty-five and thirty-seven years old. The *Last Judgement,* that he began working on 1536, was unveiled in 1541 when he was over sixty.

Michelangelo's most famous personal and artistic achievements fall within this time span (1508-1541): the *Slaves* for the never-completed tomb of Pope Julius II, the tomb sculptures in the New Sacristy in the Basilica of San Lorenzo, in Florence, and his political commitment – democratic republican spirit that he was – to defend his besieged city (1530) from the imperial army that wanted to reinstate the Medici autocracy. It was during this period that "his" popes played leading roles; they were Michelangelo's great patrons, and offered him the opportunities to express his art and

create his destiny and immortal fame: Julius II della Rovere and the Farnese pope, Paul III. Before talking about Michelangelo in the Sistine Chapel, we have to say something about the room that hosts his frescoes. In the beginning, there was Sixtus IV, the della Rovere pope (1471-1484), the great pontiff who brought the Renaissance to Rome, and established the strong alliance between the Church and culture that was to last for centuries. According to the pope's intentions, the building that the architect Baccio Pontelli constructed referring to the measurements of the lost Temple of Jerusalem as described in the Old Testament (*I Kings* 7:18-20) was to be the Ark of the new and definitive covenant between God and the Christian people, the place where the primacy of the Church of Rome would be affirmed and the place to celebrate the life *sub Gratia* – under grace – of Christ who transfigures and appropriates the life *sub Lege* – under law – of Moses.

In 1481 (the contract is dated 27 October of that year), Sixtus IV commissioned a group of famous Umbrian and Florentine artists (Perugino, Ghirlandaio, Botticelli, and Cosimo Rosselli helped by assistants such as Biagio d'Antonio, Bartolomeo della Gatta, and Luca Signorelli) to paint *Scenes from the Life of Christ* and *of Moses,* on the right and left walls, respectively.

View of the Sistine Chapel (1508-1512) **with the ceiling and the *Last Judgement*** (1536-1541) by Michelangelo and the fifteenth century frescoes on the side walls.

IN THE TOP REGISTER

1. Michelangelo
   Lunette, *Ancestors of Christ*,
   prince Naasson to the right
   and his future wife to the left.

2. Michelangelo
   Lunette, *Ancestors of Christ*,
   the old David and Solomon to the left,
   and Bathsheba to the right.

3. Michelangelo
   Lunette, *Ancestors of Christ*,
   Josaphat to the left, and the little Joram
   embracing his mother to the right.

4. Michelangelo
   Lunette, *Ancestors of Christ*, Meshullemeth
   cradling Amon to the left, and the repentant
   Manasseh to the right.

5. Michelangelo
   Lunette, *Ancestors of Christ*,
   Josiah and the little Jeconiah to the right
   and Salathiel with his mother to the left.

6. Michelangelo
   Lunette, *Ancestors of Christ*,
   Azor and the little Sadoch to the left,
   and a "philosopher" to the right.

7. Michelangelo
   Lunette, *Ancestors of Christ*,
   prince Aminadab to left
   and a woman combing her hair to the right.

8. Michelangelo
   Lunette, *Ancestors of Christ*, King Booz to the right
   and his wife Ruth with Obed to the left.

9. Michelangelo
   Lunette *Ancestors of Christ*,
   Abia as a child and a woman to the left,
   and a sleeping figure to the right.

10. Michelangelo
    Lunette, *Ancestors of Christ*,
    Joatham and his son Achaz to the left
    and a woman to the right.

11. Michelangelo
    Lunette, *Ancestors of Christ*,
    Zorobabel and Abiud to the right,
    and Eliakim with his mother to the left.

12. Michelangelo
    Lunette, *Ancestors of Christ*,
    Achim and Eliud to the left,
    and Eliud's mother nursing a child to the right.

on pages 17-24:

Sistine Chapel (1508-1512)
North and south walls

IN THE CENTRE REGISTER, A SERIES OF 24 POPES

1. Anacletus, Greek? (76-88)
   and Alexander I, Roman (105-115).

2. Telesphorus, Greek (126-136)
   and Pius I, from Aquileia (140-155).

3. Soter, from Fondi (166-175)
   and Victor I, African (189-199).

4. Callistus I, Roman (217-222)
   and Pontain, Roman (230-235).

5. Fabian, Roman (236-250)
   and Lucius I (?), Roman (253-254).

6. Sixtus II, Greek? (257-258)
   and Felix I, Roman (269-274).

7. Clement, Roman (88-97)
   and Evaristus, Greek (97-105).

8. Sixtus I, Roman (115-125)
   and Hyginus, Greek (136-140).

9. Anicetus, Syrian (155-166)
   and Eleutherius, from Epirus (175-189).

10. Zephyrinus, Roman (199-217)
    and Urban I, Roman (222-230).

11. Anterus, Greek (235-236)
    and Cornelius, Roman (251-253).

12. Stephen I, Roman (254-257)
    and Dionysius, Roman (259-268).

IN THE BOTTOM REGISTER, THE FIFTEENTH CENTURY FRESCOES

1. Pietro Perugino
   The Baptism of Christ
   In the background, a sermon by the Baptist
   and a sermon by Christ.

2. Sandro Botticelli
   The Temptations of Christ
   In the foreground, the *Cleansing of the Leper*
   according to the Mosaic ritual.

3. Domenico Ghirlandaio
   The Calling of Saint Peter and Saint Andrew
   In the background, Christ calls the two brothers
   and two other apostles.

4. Cosimo Rosselli
   The Sermon on the Mount
   To the right, Christ heals a leper.

5. Pietro Perugino
   The Giving of the Keys to Saint Peter
   In the background, the scene of the tribute money
   and the attempted stoning of Christ.

6. Cosimo Rosselli
   The Last Supper
   In the background, beyond the windows:
   the Agony in the Garden, the Kiss of Judas
   and the Crucifixion.

7. Pietro Perugino
   Moses' Journey into Egypt
   Having taken leave of Jethro (background),
   Moses is stopped by an angel (foreground).
   To the right, Zipporah circumcises Moses' son.

8. Sandro Botticelli
   The Trials of Moses
   Having fled from the pharaoh, Moses defends Jethro's
   daughters at the well. Pasturing the flock
   on Mount Horeb, he listens to God's command and,
   with his family, departs for Egypt.

9. Biagio di Antonio
   Crossing of the Red Sea
   The Israelites are safe on the shore,
   while the waters close over pharaoh's army.

10. Cosimo Rosselli
    The Descent from Mount Sinai
    w *Adoration of the Golden Calf*
    Moses receives the Tables of the Law from God
    on Mount Sinai (top), and having come down
    from the mountain shows them to the people.
    Enraged, he breaks them and punishes those who had
    worshipped the golden calf (top right).

11. Sandro Botticelli
    Punishment of Korah, Dathan and Abiram,
    Moses put them to the test, and the confused rebels
    are swallowed by the earth.

12. Luca Signorelli and Bartolomeo della Gatta
    The Last Acts of Moses
    The Lawgiver reiterates the law, and after having
    seen the Promised Land from Mount Nebo, he comes
    down and gives the rod to Joshua. In the background,
    to the left, the death of Moses.

CVMAEA

EZECHIAS
MANASSES
AMON

ESAIAS

IOSIAS
IECHONIAS
SALATHIEL

PROMVLGATIO·EVANGELICÆ·LEGIS·PERCHRISTVM   4   CONTVRBATIO·IESV·CHISIS   5

ERITHRAEA

ZOROBABEL
ABIVD
ELIACHIM

OZIAS
IOATHAM
ACHAZ

·BATIO·MOISI· **11** ·IS·SCRIPTAE·LATORIS· ❧ ·PROMVLGATIO·LEGIS· **10** ·SCRIPTE·PER·N·

IACOB
IOSEPH

ACHIM
ELIVD

IOEL

REPLICATIO·LEGIS·SCRIPTAE·AMOISE·CONTVR

DELPHICA

AZOR
SADOCH

...TI·LEGISLATORIS · ✠ · REPLICATIO·LEGIS·EVANGELICAE·A·CHRISTO

6

EZECHIEL

ROBOAM
ABIAS

PERSICHA

SALM
BOC
OB

·MOISEM· CONGREGATIO·POPVLI·9·MOISE·LEGEM·SCRIPTAM·ACCEPTVRI·TEMPTATIO·MOISI·L

LIBICA

NAASON

INSTITVTIO NOVAE REGENERATIONIS A CHRISTO IN BAPTISMO

TEMPTATIO IES

HIEREMIAS

AMINADAB

SIXTVS·ROMANVS·SE·ANX
MIID·XX·I·MAR·CORONAT
VR·ANX·PI·C·   ·P·AMII·D·XXIII·

S·EVARETVS·GRECVS·PAT
RE·IVD·OEX·BETHLEEM·
SE·AN·XIIII·X·DI·MARTO
RON·ATVR·AN·

S·CLEMENS·ROMANVS·SEDIT
AN·VIII·MIID·XX·IIAR·CORON
ATVR·AN·XPI·C·

GIS·SCRIPTAE·LATORIS   OBSERVATIO·ANTIQVE·REGENERATIONIS·A·MOISE·PER·CIRCONCISIONEM

The fifteenth century Sistine Chapel as we see it today consists of twelve panels, six on each wall. These are in the median section, because the upper register along the two walls is decorated with a sequence of twenty-eight full-length images of Peter's successors in mock niches.

Originally, the series of pontiffs started from the back wall where Michelangelo would later paint the *Last Judgement*. There were Christ with Peter, with Linus and with Cletus, the first popes in the succession of Vicars. In the centre was Pietro Perugino's masterpiece, the *Assumption of the Virgin* that was also demolished

to allow Buonarroti to paint his huge fresco.

Originally there were more scenes along the walls, sixteen instead of the twelve we see today. The four, painted on the wall where the *Last Judgement* is now and on the entrance wall (the *Finding of Moses*, the *Birth of Jesus*, the *Resurrection of Christ*, the *Dispute over the Body of Moses*) have all been destroyed: the first two to make room for Michelangelo and the other two were lost due to a structural failure in 1522. Only the *Resurrection of Christ* and the *Dispute over the Body of Moses* on the entrance wall were replicated in the late-Mannerist style by Hendrick

van der Broeck and Matteo di Lecce during the sixteenth century.

The iconographic arrangement of the fifteenth century Sistine chapel is perfectly clear. Moses and Christ are the two lawgivers: Moses who gave the Old Testament and Jesus the New. The first law is the prefiguration and prophecy of the second, last and definitive law that Christ established and which the Church protects and administers in the legitimacy of the apostolic succession (the series of popes that began with Peter, the vicar).

It is certainly no accident, nor is it without significance that *The Giving of the Keys to Saint Peter* by Pietro Perugino is

on page 25:
Interior of the Sistine Chapel,
engraving by Ugo Tonietti (1508)

The ceiling with the starry night sky by Pier Matteo d'Amelia, prior to Michelangelo's frescoes. On the back wall are the paintings and two windows that were eliminated to make room for the *Last Judgement*.

Outside view of the Sistine Chapel

from the left:
Domenico Ghirlandaio
Pope Saint Caius (1481)

Sandro Botticelli
Pope Saint Marcellinus (1481)
Detail of the central register, above the fifteenth century frescoes in the Sistine Chapel.

The Sistine painters brought perspective, naturalism, illusionism, an understanding of composition, scenography and colour, the infinite – and infinitely seductive – world of visible beauty and human character, emotions and affections into the Vatican. The visitors who, knowing nothing of the history of art, enter the Sistine Chapel for the first time, could think that centuries separate the style of the ceiling and *Last Judgement* and the style of the fifteenth century panels to the point that they will see Michelangelo as radically new and totally incomparable to his predecessors. My advice is to dedicate sufficient time to Botticelli, Perugino, Ghirlandaio and all the other Tuscan and Umbrian masters who worked in the Sistine Chapel during the fifteenth century without being immediately entranced by Michelangelo. Also because the best way to understand Buonarroti's style is to first comprehend the cultural context from which he started. In fact, it was this aggregate of excellence, from Domenico Ghirlandaio, to whom Michelangelo was apprenticed as a child, to Botticelli and Perugino whom he had occasion to meet during his life, that triggered the dizzying acceleration which, in barely twenty-five years, from 1483 to 1508, led to the frescoes on the ceiling.

the first image that strikes the eyes of anyone who enters the Sistine Chapel from the Sala Regia (Regal Room). Two monumental figures face each other, standing in a square that is as vast and ancient as the majesty of Rome and amplified by a sharp perspective that focuses on the central plan building in the background. One is Christ giving the Vicar the keys to the Kingdom, the other is the kneeling Peter who receives them. The entire Gospel episode of *"Tibi dabo claves"* is harmony, solemnity and rapt silence. The primacy of Peter and hence of the Roman pontiffs – the rock on which the Universal Church stands and fundamental theo-

logical key to understanding the iconography of the fifteenth century Sistine Chapel – is depicted with majestic simplicity and impressive naturalness.
We can say that the Renaissance entered Rome on 15 August 1483, the Feast of the Assumption of the Virgin Mary, when the pope unveiled the newly finished painting cycle, with the still fresh plaster. The twelve immense panels, arranged in a way that creates a homology and balance among them without, however, quashing the individual artists' stylistic characteristics or variations, comprise a choral piece the likes of which had never before been seen in Rome.

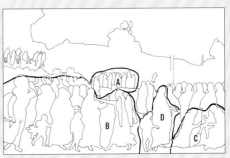

Pietro Perugino
Moses' Journey into Egypt

The title at the top: «Moses Observes the Old Rule
of Regeneration through Circumcision».
The fresco illustrates the episode from *Exodus* (4:18-20):
Moses, having received Yahweh's command, takes leave
of his father-in-law Jethro **(A)** and with his wife Zipporah,
his sons Gershom and Eliezer and retinue, sets out for Egypt.
And along the road, the Angel "came to him… and tried
to kill him" (*Ex.* 4:24) **(B)**. Zipporah circumcises Eliezer **(C)**
as Moses and his first-born son look on **(D)**. The covenant
with the Lord is confirmed and Moses' mission
is consecrated. The identities of the figures are uncertain.
Some maintain that the youth behind Moses stopped
by the angel is a portrait of Pinturicchio.

Sandro Botticelli
The Trials of Moses

The title at the top: «Temptation of Moses, Promulgator of the Written Law». The fresco depicts the scenes from Exodus (2, 3, 4): Moses kills an Egyptian who had attacked a Jew (**A**), while a woman helps the beaten man (**B**). He flees to Midian (**C**) where he chases away the shepherds who prevent Jethro's daughters from watering their flock (**D**) and helps the girls (**E**). Grazing his father-in-law's flocks he hears Yahweh calling him on Mount Horeb. He removes his shoes and approaches the burning bush (**F**) and is ordered to return to Egypt to free the Israelites (**G**). Armed with the rod of Yahweh, he sets off for Egypt with his wife Zipporah and his sons (**H**).

on the following pages:
Sandro Botticelli
The Trials of Moses, detail

Moses helps Jethro's daughters water their flock.

Biagio di Antonio
Crossing of the Red Sea, detail

Pharaoh's soldiers drown in the sea as Moses commands the waters with his rod.

TEMPTATIO · MO

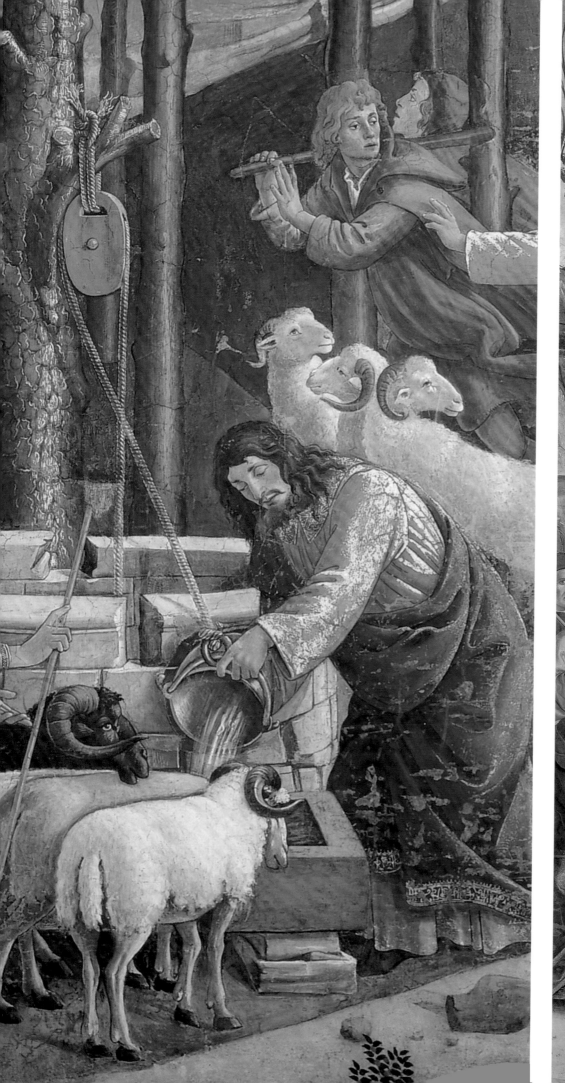

Biagio di Antonio
Crossing of the Red Sea

The title at the top: «Moses Gathers the People who will Receive the Written Law». In the background to the right, the pharaoh on his throne takes counsel on the flight of the Jews **(A)** and in the foreground, his horsemen are drowned in the waters **(B)**. To the left, Moses on the shore, surrounded by the Israelites, commands the waves with his rod, while the people sing the song of thanksgiving to Yahweh (*Ex.* 14:27, 28; 15:1) **(C)**. Among the figures to the right of Moses is a portrait of Cardinal Bessarione wearing a red and white mantle and holding a reliquary; he brought the relic of Saint Andrew's head to Rome and, in the 15th century, was a great supporter of the crusade against the Turks and of the union of the churches.

Cosimo Rosselli
The Descent from Mount Sinai
and detail

The title at the top: «Promulgation of the Written Law Through Moses» (*Ex.* 31, 32, 33). On Mount Sinai, God gives Moses the Ten Commandments **(A)**; Moses, down from the mountain and furious over the adoration of the golden calf, breaks the Tables of the Law **(B)** and harshly punishes those guilty of idolatry **(C)**. He goes back up onto the mountain and descends with the new Tables that he shows to the people dazzled by the splendour of his face **(D)**. The portraits and landscapes are by Rosselli's Florentine helper, Piero di Cosimo.

Sandro Botticelli
Punishment of Korah, Dathan and Abiram

The title at the top reads: «Rebellion against Moses the Lawgiver». Korah, Dathan and Abiram who, with their followers, had rebelled against Moses (**A**) refusing his authority and wanting usurp Aaron's priestly office, are put to the test. Before the altar, the prophet invokes the help of Yaweh against the rebels (**B**), while their censers fall to the ground (**C**). Only Aaron is accepted (**D**). Cursed by God, the rebels are swallowed by the earth (**E**) (*Num.* 16:1 ff.) and their 250 followers are devoured by fire (*Num.* 16:31-35). The building to the right (**F**) is the Septizodium, that was still standing in the day of Sixtus IV; the inscription on the Arch of Constantine in the centre (**G**) reads: «Let no one take the honour (of the High Priesthood) if he is not called by God». The second figure at the far right may be Botticelli.

NEMO · SIBI · ASSVMM
AT HONOREM · NISI
VOCATVS · ADEO
TANQVAM · ARON

SCRIPTAE · AMO

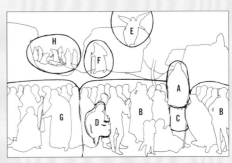

Luca Signorelli and Bartolomeo della Gatta
The Last Acts of Moses

The title at the top: «Repetition of the Written Law by Moses». Close to the end of his life, the prophet, seated on a throne (**A**) holding the book of the Law, repeats the Law and entrusts it to the listening people (**B**). At his feet, in a chest, the Tables of the Law and the bowl of manna (**C**). The nude youth (**D**) in the centre may symbolize the tribe of Levi that were not given part of the Promised Land because they were to live only from the proceeds of worship. At the top, Moses on Mount Nebo looks at the Promised Land (**E**) that he will not enter. Then, descending from the mountain (**F**), he gives Joshua the rod of command (**G**) and dies (**H**) in Moab, at the age of 120 years.

Luca Signorelli
and Bartolomeo della Gatta
The Last Acts of Moses, detail
Nude youth symbolizing the tribe of Levi that
were not given part of the Promised Land.

Pietro Perugino
The Baptism of Christ, detail
Saint John the Baptist baptizes Jesus
Christ, with the dove of the Holy Spirit
hovering above His head.

Pietro Perugino
The Baptism of Christ

The title at the top, with the artist's name below: «The Institution of the New Regeneration by Christ through Baptism» and «The work of Pietro Perugino, of Città della Pieve». In the centre, the group of the Eternal Father (**A**). In the foreground, the Baptism of Christ (**B**) with the dove hovering above His head (*Matt.* 3:13 ff.). In the background, the sermon of the Precursor (**C**), the Baptist who goes down to the Jordan (**D**) and the sermon of Jesus (**E**). The identities of the figures in the central scene are uncertain.

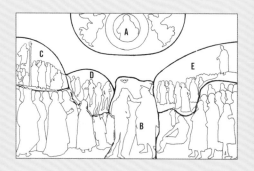

Sandro Botticelli
The Temptations of Christ
and detail of the *Cleansing of the leper*

The title at the top: «Temptation of Christ, Lawgiver of the Gospel». Satan, disguised as a Franciscan, tempts Christ who is fasting in the desert (**A**); he then takes him to the pinnacle of the Temple and tempts Him again (**B**); finally, high on a mountain, defeated for the third time, the demon throws off the habit and disappears. The angels draw near and serve the food (*Matt.* 4) (**C**). Down from the mountain, Christ watches the cleansing of the leper (**D**), whom he had healed (*Mark* 1:40). The complicated ritual takes place in the foreground (**E**), according to *Leviticus* 14:1 ff. The building in the centre is the Ospedale di Santo Spirito, built by order of Sixtus IV, the della Rovere pope; the two oak trees allude to his family. The two figures to the far left may be Botticelli and Filippino Lippi.

Domenico Ghirlandaio
The Calling of Saint Peter and Saint Andrew

The title at the top: «Gathering of the People who will
Accept the Law of the Gospel». On the Sea of Galilee,
in the midst of a solemn landscape of trees and rocks,
Jesus calls the first Apostles, Peter and his brother Andrew:
«Follow me and I will make you fishers of men»
(*Matt.* 4:18-22) **(A)**. In the foreground, they have left the
boat and follow the Messiah, and kneeling thank Him **(B)**,
while a large group of figures looks on.
In the background, to the right, Jesus calls two other
brothers to the apostolate, James and John as they are
fishing on the lake with their father Zebedee **(C)**.

Pietro Perugino
The Giving of the Keys to Saint Peter and detail

The title at the top: «Rebellion against Jesus Christ, Lawgiver». Christ, in the foreground, entrusts the keys to Peter (*Matt.* 16:19) (**A**). In the background on the broad polychrome marble pavement, the episodes of the payment of the tribute (*Matt.* 17:17 ff.) (**B**) and the attempted stoning of Christ (*John* 8:59; 10:31 ff.) (**C**). The background is dominated by a Renaissance version of the Temple of Jerusalem (**D**) and to either side, two arches imitating the Arch of Constantine (**E**) and an inscription praising Sixtus IV who emulated of Solomon for having built the Sistine Chapel which is superior, if not in riches, at least for its piety. Alfonso of Calabria (**1**), Perugino (**2**), Pinturicchio (**3**), the helper Bartolomeo della Gatta (according to others, Baccio Pontelli) (**4**) and Giovannino de' Dolci, the architect who designed the chapel (**5**) have been identified among the figures witnessing the scene.

Cosimo Rosselli
The Sermon on the Mount

Title at the top: «Promulgation of the Law of the Gospel by Christ». This is the poorest of Rosselli's four frescoes in the Sistine Chapel. The very compact crowd creates a sensation of disorder, depriving the composition of clarity. On the mountain in the distance, Christ is rapt in prayer (**A**): at the foot of the mountain He comes down to the multitude (**B**) in the foreground; in the centre, on a grassy rise He delivers the Beatitudes (**C**). At the far right, the healing of the leper (**D**) according to Matthew, chapters 4 and 8. Again, the best part of this fresco, the grandiose, wild background, is the work of Rosselli's helper, the Florentine artist, Piero di Cosimo.

Cosimo Rosselli
The Sermon on the Mount, detail
Healing of the leper.

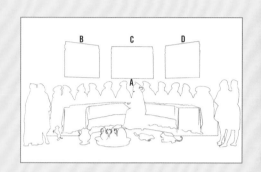

Cosimo Rosselli
The Last Supper

At the top, the title: «Repetition of the Gospel Law by Christ». **(A)** In the foreground, the Saviour, among the disciples, blesses and breaks the bread (*Matt.* 26:26) and opposite Him, Judas makes ready to leave and betray Him. Judas has a dark halo on his head and the demon on his back (*Luke* 22:3). The scenes in the background windows from the left, are: **(B)** the Agony in the Garden, **(C)** the Kiss of Judas **(D)** the Crucifixion. The identities of the four figures to the sides are unknown.

EVANGELICAE·A·CHRISTO

The Ceiling

And now we come to that fateful year of 1508, when Pope Julius II ordered Michelangelo to paint the ceiling and complete the project launched by his uncle, Sixtus IV nearly three decades earlier. The contract is dated 8 May 1508. The first part, from the entrance to the centre, was completed on 15 August 1511, and it was all finished on 31 October 1512 when, surrounded by his cardinals, the pope celebrated the solemn vespers on the eve of the Feast of all Saints in the Sistine Chapel.

In 1508, Michelangelo was thirty-three years old and famous in Rome, in Italy and beyond. It is sufficient to mention that on 8 September 1504 he had raised the statue of *David* in front of the Palazzo Vecchio in Florence.

For the first time, since the days of ancient Greece and Rome, a statue of a nude man, four times bigger than life, stood in a public square. It is the first modern sculpture in the history of art – according to Giorgio Vasari – and from that point on, there would be neither Phidias nor Polyclitus, Michelangelo had defeated the ancients.

Julius II knew this young yet very famous artist well. In February 1508, Michelangelo had cast a bronze portrait statue of the pope which, for a few brief

years stood on the façade of the Basilica of San Petronio in Bologna until it was destroyed during a popular uprising in 1512.

There had been clashes and tension between the pontiff and Buonarroti regarding the pope's tomb that was to have been placed in the heart of the new Saint Peter's Basilica. It was to be of unprecedented size and grandeur with forty sculpted figures, some of which (the famous *Slaves*), the result of new designs and adaptations made over the years, have survived to the present.

Between 1505 and 1506 Michelangelo was fully occupied selecting and ordering marble from the quarries at Carrara, but the project was aborted shortly after it was conceived. The construction of the new Saint Peter's, assigned to Donato Bramante (the first stone was laid on 18 April 1506) had taken up all the attention and resources of the Apostolic See. Michelangelo, angered over the fact that the huge project had gone up in smoke and that he had wasted his time and efforts, left Rome and only returned after repeated summonses on the part of Julius II.

The project Michelangelo began working on in May 1508 went against his nature, since he considered himself a sculptor and not a painter. And yet, he tackled the huge worksite (over one

thousand square meters to cover with fresco, more than three hundred figures) as if it were a wager with himself and with the pope.

The artist who worked uninterruptedly for four years frescoing the ceiling of the Sistine Chapel was still a man in his prime. He set to the task with a tense energy, firm determination, intolerant of helpers and assistants, and alone, as if it were a duel, a hand-to-hand fight, with the plaster that he had to fill with figures.

As everyone knows, Michelangelo was excellent at promoting his own image. Superiority, exactingness, misanthropy, surliness and a quick temper were, without a doubt, distinctive traits of his personality. He not only did nothing to hide or modify them, he cultivated them and showed them off to construct a heroic profile that was amplified in the contemporary literature: by his biographer Ascanio Condivi, and by Giorgio Vasari who, in the two editions of the *Lives* (1550 and 1568), created the historiographic legend of the "divine" Michelangelo who reached the highest peak in the centuries-old history of the arts.

We can understand what the Sistine Chapel project was and how the artist wanted to portray himself from a document (*Sonnet* 5), an autograph sheet that is conserved in the archives of Casa Buonarroti in Florence. Next

Michelangelo
**Michelangelo's drawing
of himself painting the Sistine
Ceiling, on the same page
as a sonnet**
(1511-1512).

to a caricature of himself painting in an uncomfortable position, he wrote the poem (*I'ho già facto un gozzo*):

*I've grown a goitre by dwelling in this den —
As cats from stagnant streams in Lombardy,
Or in what other land they happen to be —
Which drives the belly close beneath the chin:
My beard turns up to heaven; my nape falls in,
Fixed on my spine: my breast-bone visibly
   Grows like a harp: a rich embroidery
Bedews my face from brush-drops thick and thin.
My loins into my paunch like levers grind:
My buttock like a crupper bears my weight;
   My feet unguided wander to and fro;
In front my skin grows loose and long; behind,
By bending it becomes more taut and strait;
   Crosswise I strain me like a Syrian bow:
     Whence false and quaint, I know,
Must be the fruit of squinting brain and eye;
   For ill can aim the gun that bends awry.
     Come then, Giovanni, try
To succour my dead pictures and my fame;
Since foul I fare and painting is my shame*[3].

This sonnet, addressed to his friend Giovanni da Pistoia, is grotesque, surreal, sulphurous. It speaks of a man who is twisted and bent out of shape by his work, a man, a sculptor, who does not feel suited to painting in fresco, who is angry, disappointed, discouraged and yet, in two beautiful lines, (*a rich embroidery / Bedews my face from brush-drops thick and thin*) is able to exalt the glorious labour of art.

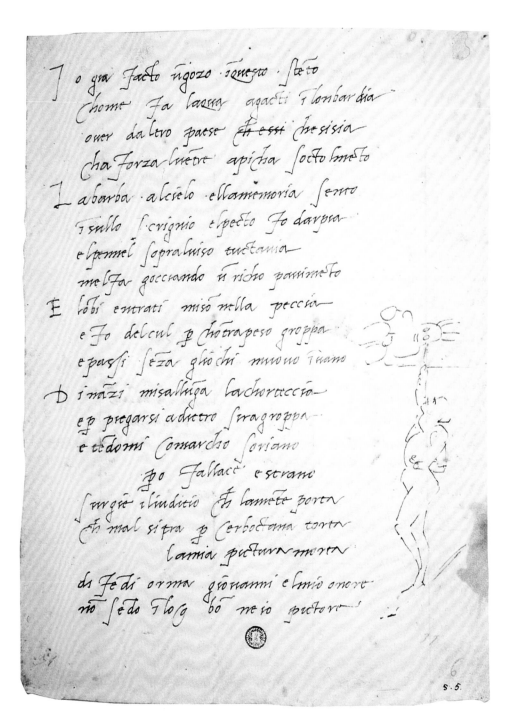

Michelangelo essentially worked alone on the scaffolding in the Sistine Chapel. He only occasionally used the services of the helpers his Florentine friends, Francesco Granacci and Giuliano Bugiardini, had found for him. He had some problems in the beginning because he had not perfectly mastered the fresco technique, but soon he found the right balance and rhythm.

Actually, Michelangelo was left free to organize the worksite and to design the ceiling as he wished, using the helpers he wanted. The 1508 contract called for an iconography that the artist radically reinvented. Within a mock architectural frame, which by itself is a masterpiece of perspective illusion, there is an amazing world of figures and episodes.

In the centre, within four large and five smaller, panels are nine episodes from *Genesis*: *The Separation of the Light from the Darkness*, *The Creation of the Stars*, *The Separation of the Earth from the Waters*, *The Creation of Adam*, *The Creation of Eve*, *The Original Sin*, *The Sacrifice of Noah*, *The Flood*, *The Drunkenness of Noah*. This is the iconographic sequence of the scenes, but they were actually painted in reverse order, since Michelangelo began his work on the part of the ceiling closest to the entrance wall.

As we look at the Sistine ceiling following the iconographic sequence, taking in the stories from *Genesis* one at a time, we realize that as we go from the back wall with *The Drunkenness of Noah* and *The Flood* (the first that were painted) towards the beginning of the Biblical story, the scenes become simpler acquiring a grandiosity of form and confidence in perspective foreshortening. We get the impression that the artist gradually realized the expressive potential of fresco and how perfectly the technique was suited to his creations.

What is astonishing in the frescoes with the scenes from *Genesis* is Michelangelo's ability to radically and brilliantly reinvent iconographies that had been established for centuries. The Eternal Father who divides light from darkness is an acrobatic figure who extends over the primeval void. He is the force of creation – on the one side the light of day and on the other, the darkness of night – and the sudden flash from which everything began. Michelangelo created the image of his concept of the big bang.

Ever since the beginning, even the greatest artists had depicted the creation of man as a more or less literal rendering of the Biblical text. God models the image of man from clay, He breathes the spirit of life into him and gives him his immortal soul and destiny. Michelangelo did away with the traditional iconography and invented another that was so new and so powerful that even five centuries later it can still trigger emotions and astonishment. There is not a trace of naïve materiality in Michelangelo's *Creation of Adam*. The first man is reclining on the ground, he comes from the earth, but what creates him is the spark released by God's index finger when it touches his, we could say, by transmitting an electric fluid. God arrives in a glorious whirl amplified by the red cape inside of which, as if sheltered by a wind-filled sail, are the angels of His retinue, personifications of the Almighty's powers. Someone, with a hypothesis that is definitely imaginative and unlikely, but still fascinating, has seen the outlines of a human brain in the group of God the Father surrounded by angels. It is almost as if the scene were the manifesto of a "creationist" Michelangelo, a precursor of "intelligent design".

The book of *Genesis* tells about the beginning of Time but time moves towards the redemption of humanity represented by the Christ who will come. The Prophets and Sibyls announce him from the depths of the centuries, the ancestors of our Lord prepare for His advent over generations. We immediately realize that a formidable and impeccable theological system governs the design of the ceiling. Even though the symbolic role of the twenty *Ignudi*, the splendid male figures holding wreaths of oak leaves that allude to the name and glory of the della Rovere pope, Julius II[4], set in the corners and seated on plinths, framing scenes of *Genesis* is not entirely comprehensible, the meaning of the twelve gigantic figures of the *Seers* is abundantly clear.

They are the images of seven Old Testament *Prophets* and five *Prophetesses* from the classical tradition. All are called up from the depths of history, from the *sub Lege*, Judaic world, and from the *ante* or *extra Legem* pagan world. They symbolize Hope and Expectation, they prophesize the Saviour who will come and for whose incarnation, the generations of *The Ancestors of Christ*, depicted in the parallel series below, are preparing.

The *Prophet Jonah* has a special place and meaning. The Bible tells us that Jonah had refused to obey the Lord's command to prophesy to the sinners of Nineveh. The sailors of the ship carrying the prophet cast him into the sea where he was swallowed by an enormous fish and, after three days, was spewed out alive on the beach.

Therefore, the prophet Jonah is the symbol of pardon and repentance, both supreme sacramental powers of the Church, but he is also a symbol of Christ who rose after three days. When Michelangelo painted the *Last Judgement* many years later, he depicted Jonah above the Resurrected Christ who,

risen from the tomb after three days like Jonah from the belly of the sea monster, comes to judge the living and the dead. And the Scriptural connection would become perfect.

At this point, let us try to consider the entire ceiling of the Sistine Chapel with its hundreds of swarming figures, the enormous project that Michelangelo completed on 30 October 1512 after four years of tireless work. In the centre, in the scenes from *Genesis* that are arranged in sequence, are the Cosmogony, the origins of Man, Original Sin, Evil bursting fatefully into history (*The Flood, The Drunkenness of Noah…*). Humanity is inexorably consigned to Wickedness, to Violence, to Death. But God does not turn His back. He intervenes to protect the Chosen People in the Biblical scenes in the pendentives at the corners of the ceiling: *The Punishment of Haman,* Assuero's minister who wanted to exterminate the Jews; *The Bronze Serpent* that Moses held up to the tribes of Israel during the Exodus to cure them of snakebites; *David and Goliath,* the young hero who killed the giant; *Judith and Holofernes,* Judith who saved her people by beheading the evil Holofernes.

God does not withdraw from History, he allows humanity to cultivate Hope and Expectation. The *Prophets* and the *Sibyls* testify to the Christ who will come in the fullness of time, while the

Ancestors of Christ slowly and laboriously prepare for His advent on earth.

The story of the Sistine Chapel could have ended in October 1512. Instead, it continued and was concluded more than a quarter of a century later when Michelangelo painted his supreme masterpiece, the *Last Judgement,* during the pontificate of Paul III Farnese, between 1536 and 1541.

By that time Italy and Europe had changed profoundly with respect to the golden age of Julius II. The Sack of Rome occurred in 1527. The spiritual unity of the West had been broken forever following the Protestant Reformation and the Catholic Church was shoring up its defences preparing for the Council of Trent, and organizing the difficult and shrewd programme of recovery that books call the Counter-Reformation. Italy was impoverished and under the control of the great powers so that with the sole exception of Venice, it was a land of limited sovereignty.

In these dramatic and calamitous times that witnessed the extinguishment of Florentine liberty after the Medici returned to power with the support of the imperial army, the sixty year old Michelangelo, the steadfast republican who had worked as a military engineer to defend his besieged Florence (1530) began preparing his last painting in the Sistine Chapel.

on pages 57-64:
Sistine Chapel. The Ceiling

Michelangelo
The Ignudi

These splendid youths, the *Ignudi*, are seated
on plinths to the sides of the five smaller compartments.
The superb creature here is on the left,
above the prophet Jeremiah's throne.

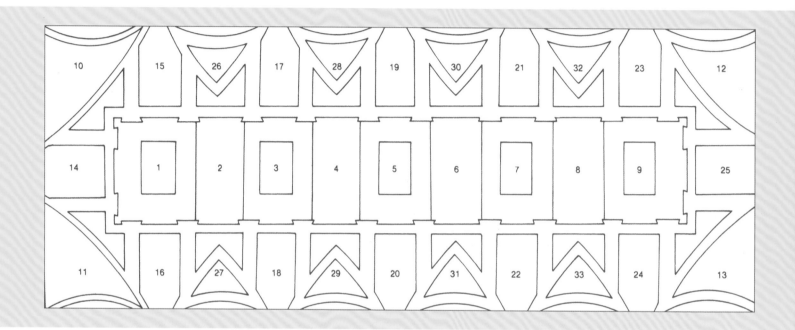

1. The Separation of the Light from the Darkness

2. The Creation of the Stars

3. The Separation of the Earth from the Waters

4. The Creation of Adam

5. The Creation of Eve

6. The Original Sin

7. The Sacrifice of Noah

8. The Flood

9. The Drunkenness of Noah

10. The Punishment of Haman

11. The Bronze Serpent

12. David and Goliath

13. Judith and Holofernes

14. The Prophet Jonah

15. The Prophet Jeremiah

16. The Libyan Sibyl

17. The Persian Sibyl

18. The Prophet Daniel

19. The Prophet Ezekiel

20. The Cumaean Sibyl

21. The Erythrean Sibyl

22. The Prophet Isaiah

23. The Prophet Joel

24. The Delphic Sybil

25. The Prophet Zechariah

26. Solomon as a child with his mother

27. The parents of the future king Jesse

28. Roboam as a child with his mother

29. Asa as a child with his father
and sleeping mother

30. Ozias as a child with his mother,
his father Joram and a brother

31. Ezekias as a child with mother
and his father, Achaz

32. Zorobabel as a child with his mother
and father, Salathiel

33. Josiah as a child with his mother,
and Amon, his father

Michelangelo
Ceiling of the Sistine Chapel
(1508-1512),
after cleaning and restoration
(1979-1994).

Michelangelo
The Separation of the Light from the Darkness
(*Gen.* 1,2).

Two pairs of *Ignudi* at the sides hold two gilded bronze shields. Above: *The Sacrifice of Isaac* (*Gen.* 22:9), and below: Elijah is taken up to heaven on a chariot of fire (2 *Kings* 2:11).

The Creation of the Stars
(*Gen.* 1:11, 16)
Here, Michelangelo painted the Creator.

on the following page:
The Creation of the Stars,
detail of God the Creator.

Michelangelo
*The Separation of the Earth
from the Waters*
(*Gen.* 1:9)

The first of the two mock gilded
bronze medallions is not historiated;
the other depicts the *Death of Absalom*
(*2 Sam.* 18:9).

on the following page:

Michelangelo
The Creation of Adam
(*Gen.* 2:7)

The powerfully expressive group with the Creator
and the first man, lying on a barren heath stands out against
the background of an empty sky. The two facing bodies
are joined by their index fingers: the decided finger
of God and the inert finger of man. The life-giving spark
flows from the arm of God.

The Sistine Chapel

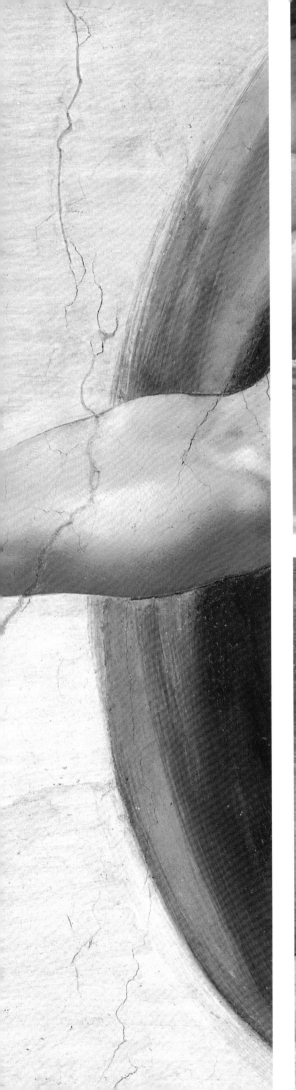

on the preceding pages:
Michelangelo
The Creation of Adam, details

Michelangelo
The Creation of Eve
(*Gen.* 2)

While Adam is deep in sleep, God brings the first woman
to life. The astounded Eve turns to Him to give thanks.
The solemn Creator, wrapped in the big cloak,
is stern and serious.

on the preceding pages:

Michelangelo
The Original Sin
(*Gen.* 3:1 ff.)

The artist depicted the two episodes, the *Temptation* and the *Expulsion* from Eden, in one frame, with the tree of life in the centre separating the scenes. It is a low fig tree, the demon is wrapped around it and, as typical throughout the Middle Ages – the upper part of his body is that of a woman. Adam picks the fruit himself, while the flattered Eve takes it from the serpent. But at the right, an angel with a sword chases Adam, and the terrified Eve crouches behind him.

Michelangelo
The Original Sin
Detail of Eve's face

Michelangelo and Raphael in the Vatican

The Sistine Chapel

Michelangelo
The Sacrifice of Noah and detail

The patriarch has left the Ark at the end of the flood
with his wife, sons and daughters-in-law; he builds an altar
and offers a burnt offering of thanks to God (*Gen.* 8:20).

on the preceding pages:

Michelangelo
The Flood

This was the first Bible story frescoed on the
ceiling: in the centre, an over laden boat risks
sinking; in the background, the ark
with the survivors seeking safety (*Gen.* 7).

Michelangelo
The Flood, details

Michelangelo
The Drunkenness of Noah

The drunken and naked Noah sleeps in front of his sons.
While Shem and Japheth cover his nakedness,
Ham in the foreground points him out to his brothers
and mocks him (*Gen.* 9:20 ff.).

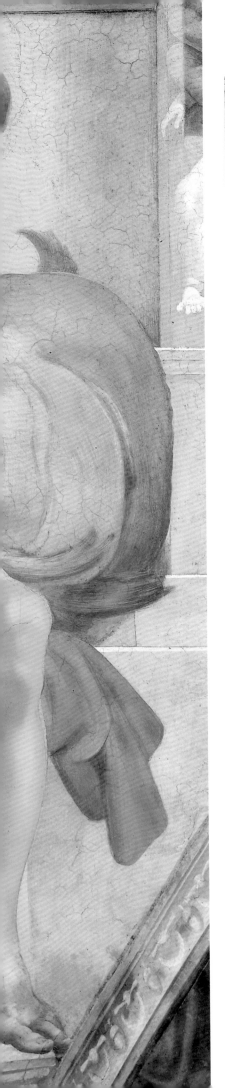

Michelangelo
The Prophet Jonah

The figure of the prophet stands above the *Last Judgement*.
To his left the whale that swallowed him and gave him up
after three days: events that herald the entombment
and resurrection of Christ.

Michelangelo
The Prophet Jeremiah

The prophet of "Lamentations"
is consumed with grief for the punishment
looming over the infidelity of Jerusalem.

LIBICA

Michelangelo
The Libyan Sibyl

With an agile movement of her body,
twisting her back and foot, this Sibyl raises
a large book to place on her knees
and prepare for the word of the oracle.

Michelangelo
The Persian Sibyl

This face, like that of the *Cumaean Sibyl*,
introduced the "monstrous" aspect
into Michelangelo's paintings.
Old and short-sighted, *The Persian Sibyl*
struggles to read the writing in the book.

PERSICHA

DANIEL

Michelangelo
The Prophet Daniel

The prophet, with his elegant
and vigorous body, is calculating
the seventy weeks before the advent
of the Anointed One.

Michelangelo
The Prophet Ezekiel

The prophet's face shows his anger about
the transgressions of his people,
and suddenly he heeds the divine warning.

EZECHIEL

Michelangelo
The Cumaean Sibyl and detail
This gigantic Sibyl, with her face ravaged by time,
is projected magnetically from the top of the figure
towards the open book in her hands
while two silent Geniuses look on.

CVMAEA

Michelangelo
The Erythrean Sibyl and detail
The pure and noble profile of this Sibyl who predicted
a future of happiness to the messenger from Rome
seems to glow with visions of sweetness.

on the following pages:
Michelangelo
The Prophet Isaiah

The breath of the Spirit fills Isaiah's cloak
in the dreamy moment that he "sees" the Virgin Mother
of the "God with us".

Michelangelo
The Prophet Joel

The prophet's careful eye looks at the scroll
of the prophecy. It may be that Michelangelo
immortalized Bramante's features
in this bald prophet with the broad forehead.

ESAIAS

IOEL

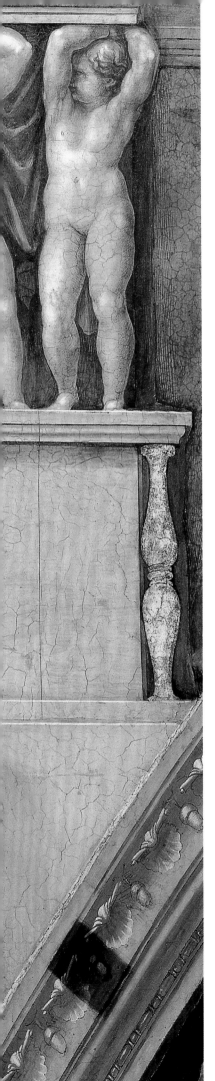

Michelangelo
The Delphic Sibyl

Admired for her physical beauty, this Sibyl, with her expanded mantle, is captured in a moment of intense inspiration with her eyes focused afar.

Michelangelo
The Prophet Zechariah

This Prophet is the first in the group of Seers. He is immobile as he reads, and is intent on "seeing" the humble Messiah-King enter into Jerusalem.

The Sistine Chapel

AMINADAB

Michelangelo
Corner spandrel with
The Punishment of Haman

Michelangelo
Corner spandrel with *The Bronze Serpent*

Michelangelo
Corner spandrel with *David and Goliath*

Michelangelo
Corner spandrel with *Judith and Holofernes*
and detail

Michelangelo
Lunette with *Azor*

Michelangelo
Lunette with *Asa,
Josaphat and Joram*

Michelangelo
Lunette with *Zorobabel,
Abiud and Eliakim*

Michelangelo
Lunette with *Achim and Eliud*

Michelangelo
Lunette with *Ezekias, Manasseh and Amon*

on the following pages:
Michelangelo
Lunette with *Eleazar*, detail

above:
Michelangelo
Ozias with his mother, father and brother,
detail of the spandrel above *Ozias*

below:
Michelangelo
Solomon and his mother,
detail of the spandrel above *Solomon*

The *Last Judgement*

Michelangelo worked on the *Last Judgement* for five years, from 1536 to 1541. The iconographic theme was compulsory in a certain sense. If the Sistine Chapel as a whole tells the story and destiny of Man created by God and entrusted to the redeeming leadership of the Church – after *Genesis*, after the establishment of the Law of Christ that embraces and goes beyond the Law of Moses, after the series of popes who by divine mandate have the authority of the keys and hence the power to bind and to loose – after all this, it would not have been complete without the *Last Judgement,* the end of the history for one and all.

This great fresco is known worldwide as the *Last Judgement.* This is correct, but it would be more appropriate to call it *Parousia* the Greek word that means the Second Coming of Christ, to judge the living and the dead, to cancel Time and History forever.

Whoever looks at the *Last Judgement* has the impression that there is no wall, but that the gaze opens onto an indefinite space of cold, blue air. It is in this unrealistic, metaphysical dimension, where Time is no longer because History has ended, that the Resurrection of the Bodies, the Judgement, Hell and Paradise all come together.

"And he that sat on the throne, said: Behold, I make all things new. And he said to me: Write, for these words are most faithful and true. And he said to me: It is done. I am Alpha and Omega; the beginning and the end (*Ap.* 21:5-6). Michelangelo's *Christ the Judge* does not sit on a throne. He is beardless, with His right hand raised in the *allocutio* gesture as an orator. He looks like a young, glorious and triumphant athlete, and yet the painter succeeded in rendering the theological anguish of the *Parousia* with extraordinary effectiveness. Time has ended, there is no more History, there is no room for mercy and forgiveness. Even the Church has completed its duty. Peter returns to Christ the keys that Jesus had given him, just as Perugino had portrayed many years before. Not even the Virgin Mary has a role any longer. She resignedly stands next to her Son because her duties as Mother of Mercy, Door of Heaven, Queen of Sinners and the Afflicted are definitively over now that everything is ended, now that everything has been decided.

The sensation triggered when we look at Michelangelo's grand mural is almost terrifying in its intensity. It is the sensation that Pope Paul III must have felt when – as the chronicles tell us – he fell to his knees overwhelmed and with tears in his eyes that last day of October, on the eve of All Saints'

Day, 1541 when the *Last Judgement* was unveiled.

There are some iconographic keys that are essential for an understanding of the *Last Judgement.* The focus of the composition, almost the engine that fires the terrible machine, is the group of *Trumpet Blowing Angels* who summon the bodies to the Resurrection. It is a tangle of young nudes who hold two open books, the small one summoning the just to Paradise, and the big one condemning the damned to Hell. Because, many are called, but only a few are the elect.

A throng of Angels at the top of the fresco presents the instruments of the Passion of Christ as testimonial evidence to the court of the Last Judgement: the cross, the column of the flagellation, the crown of thorns, and the sponge. It is because Christ died for us, shed His blood for us, that we will be judged. It is by our faith in the Cross that we will be saved or damned. This is what the display of the symbols of the Passion means to tell us.

The Church Triumphant is arranged around the heavenly Judge in a hemicycle. There is the anamorphic, caricatural self-portrait of the artist in the flayed skin – symbol of his martyrdom – that Saint Bartholomew holds in his hand. There are the angels and demons who battle over the resurrected. There is the furnace of Hell that boils and blazes through the cracks in the earth.

And then there the *Nudes*, an endless portrayal of beauty and the glory of the human body to upset and to embarrass the more devout spirits. Because this is precisely what happened – and we know it from documents and chronicles – when the *Last Judgement* was made public.

We come before the supreme tribunal of God naked, in the flower of youth and physical form, to return to the Almighty the splendour of the likeness that He Himself gave us by making us in His own image. This is unimpeachable from the theological standpoint. However, it does not mean that such a blatant display of breasts, buttocks and genitals was not very disturbing and unacceptable to many.

The successor to Paul III (who died in 1548) subtly tried to advise Michelangelo to conceal all that nudity in some way. As Giorgio Vasari tells us, the artist's ironic and scornful reply: "Tell the Pope that it is no great affair, and that it can be altered with ease. Let him put the world right, and every picture will be put right in a moment"[5] became famous. It seems that this was the artist's answer to the pope's emissary.

In fact, no one dared to touch Michelangelo's masterpiece while he was alive. It was only after his death (1564) that the parts that were or could have seemed most "scandalous" were covered with repainting and draperies.

The thankless task went to Daniele da Volterra, an excellent artist who was dubbed "Braghettone" [the breeches maker] a nickname that unjustly affected his reputation forever.

Michelangelo's *Last Judgement* has been studied, written about and celebrated in all the languages of the world. There are enough written works about it to fill a library. The comment I find most eloquent and defining is what a bizarre Florentine spirit, Anton Francesco Doni, a friend of the artist, wrote in a letter dated 1543, two years after the fresco was unveiled. In essence, Doni said, "when the Last Judgement comes, the real one, our Lord will have to abide by what Michelangelo painted because not even He could envision a better one" This hyperbolic paradox, bordering on irreverence, is the most brilliant comment ever made about the *Last Judgement*.

We all know that between 1979 and 1999, the Sistine Chapel underwent a major restoration that enthused and divided scholars and public opinion around the world. Directed by Fabrizio Mancinelli, Gianluigi Colalucci first worked on the two scenes on the entrance wall, then on the complete cycle of the *Portraits of Popes* and the *Sibyls* (1980-1984), next on the ceiling with the scenes from *Genesis* (1985-1989), and finally on the *Last Judgement* (1990-1994). The solemn mass celebrated by Pope John Paul II on 8 April 1994 marked the conclusion of the most sensational, most contested and most admired restoration of the last century. Immediately afterwards, (1995-1999) the fifteenth century paintings, that is the murals by Perugino, Ghirlandaio, Botticelli and the others were also restored for understandable reasons of homogeneity of the overall tone. The end result can now be considered one of the greatest and most successful achievements of the twentieth century.

Today, the Sistine Chapel has to deal with its global success. Visited by more than five million people each year, the nearly 2,500 square meters of the world's most famous murals are subjected to incredible stresses. The multitudes that come to Rome from all over the world to be able to say that, at least once in their lives, they saw the Sistine chapel, bring dusts, moisture and carbon dioxide – agents which over the long term are dangerous for the proper conservation of the frescoes. Preventive measures as well as ordinary and special maintenance procedures are necessary. The Office of the Conservator of the Vatican Museums takes care of this with scheduled periodic examinations of the paintings. In the meantime, the department is planning and will soon implement new technological measures that will guarantee better air circulation, decrease pollutants and offer more effective temperature and humidity control.

on pages 113-120:

The Sistine Chapel
Last Judgement
(1536-1541)
and details

A ANGELS, CHRIST AND THE CHOSEN

1. Jesus Christ
2. The Virgin Mary
3. Saint Lawrence (holding the gridiron)
4. Saint Andrew (holding the X-shaped cross)
5. Saint John the Baptist (with the fur loincloth)
6. A mother and daughter
7. Angels carrying the Cross
8. Angels carrying the Column
9. Saint Paul (with the red pallium)

10. Saint Peter (holding the big keys)
11. Saint Bartholomew (holding the knife)
12. Saint Bartholomew's flayed skin
    (with the grieved face of Michelangelo)
13. Saint Simon the Zealot (with the saw)
14. Dismas, the good thief (with the cross)
15. Saint Blaise (holding with the iron combs)
16. Saint Catherine of Alexandria
    (with the spiked wheel)
17. Saint Sebastian (with the arrows)
18. Simon, the Cyrenian (with the Cross)

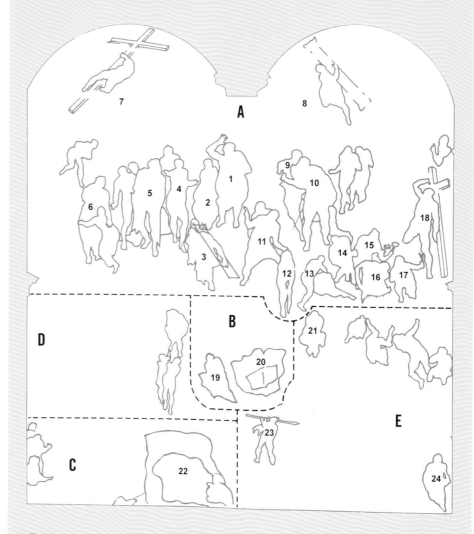

B ANGELS WITH TRUMPETS AND BOOKS

19. The book of merits
20. The book of sins

C RESURRECTION OF THE DEAD

D THE SAVED ASCENDING TO HEAVEN

E THE DAMNED BEING DRAGGED TO HELL

21. The "wretched one"
22. Lair of the demons
23. Charon
24. Minos (portrait of Biagio da Cesena)

on page 113:

Last Judgement, detail
Christ the Judge and the Virgin Mary.

Michelangelo
Last Judgement
(1536-1541), details
Angels with the instruments of the Passion.

To the sound of trumpets, angels holding the books
of merits and sins call souls to Judgement.

Michelangelo
Last Judgement, detail
Demons drag one of the damned to hell.

Michelangelo
Last Judgement, detail
The resurrected ascend to heaven.

on the following pages:
Michelangelo
Last Judgement, detail

To the right of Christ, among a group of the Blessed,
Saint Bartholomew shows the Judge the knife
of his martyrdom and flayed skin where Michelangelo
painted his self-portrait in the folds.

Michelangelo
Last Judgement, detail

Saint Blaise and Saint Catherine of Alexandria.

The Sistine Chapel

on the preceding pages:

Michelangelo
Last Judgement, detail
The demon Charon ferries souls to hell; Minos,
(a caricature of Biagio da Cesena) with his eel-tail
and ass's ears waits for them at the far right.

Last Judgement, detail
Among a group of the Blessed, Saint John
the Baptist (or Adam), to the left of the Virgin,
awaits the sentence of the Divine Judge.

Last Judgement, detail
Saint Peter holding the keys
of the Church.

Michelangelo and Raphael in the Vatican

The Pauline Chapel

Michelangelo had barely finished the *Last Judgement* when Pope Paul III summoned him to paint the *Stories of Saints Peter and Paul* in the chapel of the Palazzi Apostolici that is called Pauline after the pope.

Not part of the museum itinerary, the Pauline Chapel can only be seen on request. It has always been the most private and most intimate of all the places of worship in the Palazzi Apostolici, and it is the chapel which, even more than the Sistine, represents the mission and destiny of the Universal Church. Indeed, it is dedicated to Saints Peter and Paul. The first is the foundation of the historical and juridical legitimacy of the Roman pontiffs. The second is the cornerstone that supports and justifies the doctrine of the Church and its ecumenical mandate. When the Blessed Sacrament is exposed on the altar for adoration, the theological message protected and represented by the pope of Rome, is perfectly and efficaciously conveyed.

Therefore, the spiritual meaning and symbolic value of the *parva* (small) chapel, to distinguish it from the *magna* (big) Sistine Chapel is extraordinary. In the beginning, between 1537 and 1542, under the pontificate of Paul III, the architect Antonio da Sangallo was appointed to design the building, while Perin del Vaga was commissioned to do the stuccowork which was taken down at the end of the sixteenth century under Pope Gregory XIII.

Michelangelo probably received the commission to decorate the new chapel more or less when he completed work on the *Last Judgement*. He began by painting the *Conversion of Saint Paul*, between the end of 1542 and July 1545 on the left side as we enter, and then from 1545 to 1550, the *Crucifixion of Saint Peter* on the right wall.

The years of the Pauline Chapel were a difficult time for Buonarroti who was also involved with the Saint Peter's worksite, designing the dome, getting on in years and in poor health. Documents speak of massive purchases of ultramarine blue, and of long interruptions (in the summer of 1544 and the summer of 1546) due to the master's illnesses. Michelangelo completed his commitment in 1550.

Work in the Pauline Chapel came to a standstill that lasted for more than twenty years. The strong and decisive impetus came from Pope Gregory XIII who reigned from 1572 to 1585, the man who reformed the civil calendar, commissioned the Tower of the Winds and the Gallery of Maps (built in 1578-1580).

During his pontificate, the fresco painters Lorenzo Sabatini and Federico Zuccari, helped by a host of modellers, gilders and decorators, completed the Pauline Chapel as we see it today, with salient

The Pauline Chapel
(1542-1550)

episodes from the lives of the apostles Saint Peter and Saint Paul.

The recent general restorations of the Pauline Chapel, by the specialists of the Musei Vaticani, supervised by Maurizio De Luca and unveiled by Pope Benedict XVI on 4 July 2009, revealed a sorrowful and tragic Michelangelo, yet an artist of extraordinary plastic strength and unwavering in his command of colour. The colours are those of the *Last Judgement* and they describe a dreadful, violent and desperate humanity. Never before had Michelangelo's paintings depicted faces so distorted by stupidity and hate, such disjointed and eccentric postures, such a grand display of feral energy and obscuration of reason. Only Goya, when he painted the *Black Paintings* and the *Quinta del sordo* more than two centuries later, would be capable of working in these unsettling registers. It almost seems as if the painter were questioning himself about the theological enigma of Salvation mysteriously offered to an undeserving humanity, steeped in Evil and riddled with sin as depicted here. Michelangelo wonders about it and we have the impression that Saint Peter does too, as he looks at us, furious, in the instant that he is hoisted head down on the cross – almost as if he has doubts about the utility of his martyrdom.

As we know, that terrible idea would also fascinate another Michelangelo, Merisi da Caravaggio, who repeated it fifty years later in his painting for the Cerasi Chapel in the church of Santa Maria del Popolo in Rome.

Saint Peter gives himself freely to the cross (the restorations revealed that nail marks were added afterwards), his martyrdom is an offering.

His eyes are turned to the onlookers, but also to the door through which the pope enters. It is almost as of the Vicar wants to tell his successor: "*Tu es Petrus*", remember that the Cross is your glory and your destiny.

Michelangelo
Conversion of Saint Paul
(1542-1545)
Pauline Chapel

The Pauline Chapel

Michelangelo
Crucifixion of Saint Peter
(1548-1550), detail

Michelangelo
Crucifixion of Saint Peter
(1548-1550), detail

Michelangelo
Conversion of Saint Paul
(1542-1545), detail

Saul, blinded by the Divine Light is helped
by a companion. The seventy-year old Michelangelo
used his own features to depict the torment
in the aged face of Saul-Paul with the flowing beard.

Michelangelo
Conversion of Saint Paul
(1542-1545), detail

The Dome
of Saint Peter's

For men and women throughout world, Michelangelo in the Vatican is the Sistine Chapel, but even more so, there is the dome, the symbol of Rome and the emblem of Catholicism that bears his name.

The famous sonnet (*L'illuminazione de la cupola*, no. 1155) dated 4 April 1834, by Giuseppe Gioachino Belli, the great Italian poet who wrote in Roman dialect, comes to mind:

What people and what king have
a dome in their home, like ours
of Saint Peter's in the Vatican?
In what other city is there
a light such as this that astounds
and takes your breath away?

Belli was right. The Dome that dominates the Rome skyline, that gives the impression of covering all Christian peoples with its shadow like a mountain, changes colour with the time of day and the passage of the seasons. It is something that triggers emotions and astonishment.

The dome was Michelangelo's final project. He dedicated his remaining strength, determinedly struggling against a lack of financial resources, bureaucratic red tape, hostility, jealousy and incomprehension.

There is a document that is a masterpiece of both treachery and stupidity. In the spring of 1547 Michelangelo had been officially in charge of the Saint Peter's worksite for a few months. But there were people working against him. The great architect had powerful enemies in the Vatican government. Two officials of the Fabbrica di San Pietro, Giovanni Arborino and Antonio Massimi, could not tolerate the fact that Buonarroti went ahead without even consulting them. They tried to put him in a poor light with the pope, accusing him of wanting to radically modify Sangallo's designs (which was the truth), of demolishing parts that were already built and of incurring enormous additional costs. They wanted the pope to revoke his commission and remove him from the job.

Fortunately, Paul III treated the officials harshly and confirmed his confidence in Michelangelo. Even if the Farnese pope had not done any other good deed (and he did many during his difficult pontificate squeezed between the Protestant Reformation and the Catholic Counter-Reformation), his providential act favouring Michelangelo would have been enough to earn him the eternal gratitude of generations to come.

Michelangelo never saw the Dome rise against the Roman sky. He supervised the construction of the 1:15 scale model made of lime wood by the carpenter Battista da Carrara and monitored the construction work up to the drum.

**The inside of the Dome
of Saint Peter's Basilica**
(1546-1564 and 1588-1590)
The dome is 136.57 metres high from the floor to top of the cross and the inside diameter is 42.56 metres.

The Dome itself was built twenty years after Michelangelo's death by Giacomo della Porta who worked together with Domenico Fontana, from 1588 to 1590, and succeeded in completing the ovoid, double-shell dome which differs from the original design, in just twenty-two months thanks to the efforts of eight hundred workers. The huge gilded bronze sphere surmounted by a cross by Sebastiano Torrigiano was placed atop the lantern on 18 November 1593.

During the final years of his life, while he was busy designing the dome, Michelangelo returned to sculpting and to the theme that had intrigued his youth.

The *Rondanini Pietà* now conserved in the Museo del Castello Sforzesco in Milan, is Michelangelo's last piece, the sculpture he was still working on the eve of his death. "It is his spiritual legacy", and this phrase, spoken and written in all the languages of the world to the point that it seems a cliché, is actually the truth. A very old man, almost ninety years old, approaching the end of his life, Michelangelo caressed and tormented the *Pietà*, the silent phantasm of his final days. He devoted his last artistic thoughts to it, thoughts which were also, and above all, in that winter of 1564, religious. His final chisel strokes were for the Milan *Pietà*.

The first notice about this statue that concluded both Michelangelo's life and his artistic career in Rome, came from his pupil Daniele da Volterra. Michelangelo had been dead barely one month and on 17 March Daniele wrote to Giorgio Vasari: "We found three marble statues that he had begun… one a Man of Sorrows in Our Lady's arms… he had worked all day Saturday, and had fallen ill by Monday". A few months later, on 11 June, writing to Leonardo Buonarroti, the artist's nephew in Florence, his recollections became more precise and sorrowful: "I do not remember whether, in all that I wrote, I mentioned that Michelangelo worked throughout the whole Satur-

Giorgio Vasari
*The Construction
of the Dome of Saint Peter's*
(1546), fresco
Rome, Palazzo della Cancelleria,
Sala dei Cento Giorni

Michelangelo Buonarroti
and Luigi Vanvitelli
**Wooden Model
of the Dome of Saint Peter's**

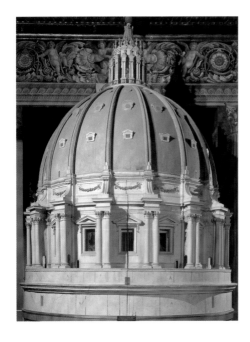

day before the first Sunday of Carnival; and he worked on his feet, studying the body of the Pietà".

The Saturday before the first Sunday of Carnival, on the eve of the illness that would soon take him away forever. the great old man faced his final duel with art. "On his feet", wrote Daniele da Volterra, and "studying". The choice of words was not random. "On his feet" because the confrontation with the work of art is a fiery attack; "studying" in the sense that for Michelangelo figurative expression was also, and up to the last, research, mental anger and untiring experimentation.

As we know, the creation of the *Rondanini Pietà* was a long and painstaking process, with continuous remodelling. Michelangelo worked on it between 1550 and 1564, with long pauses, making frequent changes and corrections.

The *Pietà* had not been commissioned by any patrons, neither was it destined for public display. It was a statue that Michelangelo carved for himself, as Giorgio Vasari wrote "… on which he might be able to pass some time every day with the chisel"[6]. I think it appropriate to mention the *Rondanini Pietà* at the end of a story that began with the *Pietà* in Saint Peter's Basilica. Nearly seventy years had passed and the concept of the re-

lationship between the Mother and her Son had undergone a process of formal rarefaction and almost spiritualization. The distinctness and the beauty of Christ's body diminish to the point of disappearing, and more and more, the Mother who holds Him becomes the Mother who covers, who absorbs, who wants to identify with her lifeless Son almost as if to return Him to the womb that generated Him.

The first – and truest – critical interpretation of the Milan statue comes from an entirely unpredictable source. The author was neither an artist nor an art historian, but an obscure bureaucrat, a minor officer of the Court of Rome. On 19 February 1564, the day after Michelangelo's death, an inventory of the items in the artist's studio was drawn up by order of the court. It was a routine matter, nothing more than a list for legal purposes, and therefore quick and brief, as customary in such cases, then as now.

But here is how that civil servant described the *Rondanini Pietà*: "Another statue begun for a Christ with another figure above it, attached together, roughed and not finished". The court officer's description was so concise (and perhaps so inexpert) that it did not even succeed in correctly identifying the iconography ("a Christ with another figure above it…"), and yet he

wrote that those roughed and unfinished figures were "attached together". "Attached together": the poetic fulcrum of the *Rondanini Pietà* is all here, in that body of Christ that clinging to the Virgin Mary as if to disappear in her, as if to return to the maternal womb. We first met Michelangelo in the luminous youthful glory of the Vatican *Pietà* (the "miracle" Vasari wrote about), we saw him in his enormous struggle with Divinity, with the Absolute, with History in the frescoes in the Sistine and Pauline Chapels, and in the design of the Dome. Taking leave of him in front of the *Rondanini Pietà* means understanding the profound spirituality, the sense of mournful religiosity that filled his life and his art and which now, at the end of his adventure here on earth, are so aptly embodied in these lines from one of his famous later sonnets (no. 285, sent to Vasari in 1554):

*So now I recognize how laden
with error was the affectionate fantasy
that made art an idol and sovereign
to me, like all things men want in spite
of their best interests*[7].

Michelangelo
The Dome

Detail of the drum and a view of the Dome
from the Italian garden.
Michelangelo was 81 years old when, as the chief
architect he directed the work on the Vatican
Basilica and designed the immense Dome.
When he died, the dome was only completed up
to the drum, the work was finished by Giacomo
della Porta, under Sixtus V, from 1588 to 1590.
The wooden model is on view in the Vatican.

Raphael
in the Vatican

preceding page:
Polidoro da Caravaggio
Grotesque with Satyr mask
Pilaster strip IX, detail

at the beginning of the chapter:
Raphael
Self Portrait (1509)
Detail of *The School of Athens*
Room of the Segnatura

Anonymous artist, 16th-17th century
Portrait of Julius II, after Raphael
Vatican Museums, Storage

No other painter in the entire history of art, not even Michelangelo, can be considered as important as Raffaello Sanzio – Raphael – of Urbino. More than any other artist, he has truly been the "school of the world" for centuries. We can say that, passing through Annibale Carracci and Guido Reni, through Poussin and David, and through Ingres and Canova, Raphael's spirit reached Picasso. And even today, each time an artist realizes that he is looking at a world swathed in happiness, order and splendour, he seems alive and fruitful.

If Raphael gave the Western figurative artistic heritage its supreme models, it is important to know that the great majority of the archetypes that would influence the style and destiny of generations of artists is conserved in that part of Rome encircled by the Leonine Wall and known to the world as Vatican City. I am talking about the *Stanze* – the rooms – named for him, the frescoed Loggias in the Palazzo Apostolico, the series of tapestries with the *Acts of the Apostles*, and the magnificent altarpieces: the *Oddi Altarpiece*, the *Madonna of Foligno* and the *Transfiguration*.

Except for the Loggia for which special permission is needed, all of these works are part of the standard itinerary of the Vatican Museums. And all, with the sole exceptions of the *Oddi*

The Vatican Rooms

Altarpiece and the predella of the dismembered *Baglioni Altarpiece* (the central panel is now in the Galleria Borghese, Rome) depicting the three Theological Virtues, were painted in Rome between 1508 and 1520, during the reigns of two popes, first Julius II of the della Rovere family and then the Medici pope, Leo X.

It is a well-known fact that Raphael's life was short indeed: he died of a "continuous and acute fever" on 6 April 1520. He was only thirty-six years old. We have the feeling that he was aware of his fate. The few years of his glorious youth seem to be have been filled with projects, results and successes. Raphael gave the world his universal message in little over a decade (1508-1520) of uninterrupted and multiform works in Rome. Assisted by a host of artists (his was the last great artistic workshop of the Renaissance), appointed conservator of Roman Antiquities (1516),

flooded with requests from illustrious patrons, coordinator of grandiose projects confidently managing both their design and execution, he attended to archaeology and architecture, he supervised the great Loggia project (frescoed by his pupils by 1519) and oversaw the production of the Vatican tapestries (1515-1519), with an abundance of creative suggestions and ideas for the artists who were his contemporaries and, even more so, for the generations to come.

Raphael was just twenty-five years old when Pope Julius II commissioned him to fresco the walls of his private apartment, the rooms which ever since have been known throughout the world as the *Stanze*. He was very young, but he was already famous for his successes in Florence. Between 1504 and 1508, he had fascinated the artistic milieu of the Tuscan capital with a series of brilliant masterpieces: the *Madonna of the Goldfinch* in the Uffizi and the two Doni

portraits in the Galleria Palatina, just to mention a few.

In Rome, Raphael was able to count on the authoritative protection of Donato Bramante, the architect who in 1506 had launched the construction of the new Saint Peter's Basilica: they both hailed from the Marches and were also related by blood.

In any event, the young artist who began painting the pope's apartment at the end of 1508 and received his first payment from the Tesoreria Apostolica on 13 January 1509, did not need special recommendations. Everyone in Rome knew that that boy was a marvel of talent and practically the wonder of the century.

He was the standard-bearer (and Rome's intellectual elite was perfectly aware of it) of an immense artistic culture that was born in Urbino between Flemish affectations and the splendours of Piero della Francesca, developed in the school

of Pietro Perugino, and finally matured in Florence in contact with Fra Bartolomeo, the young Michelangelo, and Leonardo da Vinci. To contemporary eyes it all must have seemed much like it does to us today, the embodiment and transfiguration of the figurative language of an entire people.

Indeed, we can say – quoting Giorgio Vasari who was the first to understand that sublime eclecticism: "[Raphael of Urbino] studying the labours of the old masters and those of the modern, took the best from them, and having gathered it together, enriched the art of painting with that complete perfection which was shown in ancient times by the figures of Apelles and Zeuxis"[8].

The Vatican Rooms

Now let us analyze the works of Raphael in the rooms of Pope Julius II, starting from the beginning – that lasted from 1508 to 1511 – with the room known as the "Stanza della Segnatura". The name derives from the fact that in 1541 it was the seat of the highest court of the Holy See, the *Segnatura Gratiae et Iustitiae*. In reality, it originally housed the pope's private library. And so, we have to imagine that the books were related to the iconographic programme of the frescoes (Theology, Philosophy, Law, Aesthetics). The basic iconographical themes of the painted scenes was actually established and conceived by the pope himself, "*Ad praescriptum Iulii*", that is on direct instructions from the pontiff as Paolo Giovio, Raphael's patron, friend and biographer wrote.

Group of four stucco medallions
Pillar II, Raphael's Loggia

Room of the Segnatura

In 1507, before Raphael it was Sodoma who had worked in the room and painted a significant part of the complex ceiling decorations. When Raphael took over, he saved most of his older colleague's work, and in fact depicted him next to himself in *The School of Athens*, that is if Sodoma is indeed the older figure, as a consolidated tradition maintains, next to Raphael. It is a sign of the sensitivity and graciousness which, according to his contemporaries, were distinctive features of Raphael's personality.

We can say that, taken together, the frescoes in the Room of the Segnatura are a masterpiece of Catholic cultural anthropology. They convey a message that is extraordinary in terms of its clarity and modernity of vision and open-mindedness. Let us see how.

The room is relatively small. Standing in the middle of the antique polychrome inlaid marble floor, the visitor must realize that he is looking at a portrayal of human nature and human destiny as had never been depicted before; or, at least never, with such wisdom, such instructive effectiveness, such profound thought. Here, on the foundations of Catholic theology and Neoplatonic philosophy, we are at the apex of the Western culture that the Church of Rome embraced and made its own when it was at the height of its power and influence.

To understand the Room of the Segnatura we must first understand the general idea behind the entire decorative programme, and we can summarize it like this. The first duty of man is knowledge. And so *The School of Athens,* takes up the biggest wall, on a par with the so-called *Disputation of the Sacrament* facing it.

The wise men of antiquity are gathered in various poses, alone or in groups, against a majestic architectural background that recalls Donato Bramante's ideas for the new Saint Peter's Basilica that was under construction at the time. They are dominated by the early philosophers, Plato and Aristotle; Plato has his right arm raised to indicate world of ideas, of the supreme archetypes, while Aristotle holds his hand parallel to the ground, symbolizing the concreteness of the empirical method.

The *putti,* flanking the allegorical female figure representing *Philosophy* we see on the ceiling above the large mural, hold the epigraph: "*Causarum cognitio*". This is the aim of human knowledge: to understand and dominate the reasons for things. The philosophical currents and wisdom represented by the great minds gathered here all descend from Plato and Aristotle, the respective champions of idealistic and empirical philosophy. There is Socrates, there is Epicurus, there is Diogenes the half-naked cynical nihilist sprawled on the steps, alone and indifferent to everything. In the foreground Pythagoras gives a lesson on arithmetic and music theory to a small group of pupils among whom we can recognize the Muslim Averroes wearing a turban. Euclid, the father of geometry is explaining a theorem. He is bent over the slate on the ground and uses a compass for his demonstration. Tradition has it that Raphael actually portrayed Euclid as Donato Bramante, his friend, relative and fellow countryman, as well as his most influential protector at the papal court. To his right are the scientists of the heavens and the earth: Zoroaster with the planetarium, and Ptolemy with the terraqueous globe.

There is also an image of a "lone thinker" usually identified as the Greek philosopher Heraclitus. This portrayal of a misanthropic and surly intellectual has been recognized as a tribute to Michelangelo. In fact, the figure does not appear in the preparatory cartoon for *The School of Athens* conserved in the Biblioteca Ambrosiana in Milan, and the twentieth-century restorations have shown that the corresponding portion of the fresco was done at a later time and over fresh plaster, as if it were a last

A view of the Room of the Segnatura
with the *Parnassus* and the *School of Athens*

minute addition. If we consider that by the middle of 1511 the ceiling of the Sistine Chapel was already partially visible because it was complete from the entrance to the scene of Genesis with *The Creation of Eve*, the hypothesis of an offhanded tribute to Buonarroti by Raphael (a tribute that spoke to both the master's outstanding artistry and his eccentric personality) becomes quite plausible.

Opposite *The School of Athens*, of equal majesty and size, is the so-called *Disputation of the Sacrament* dedicated to the mystery of the Word Incarnate. *Theology,* the allegorical female figure dominating the scene, recites the Latin phrase, "*divinarum rerum notitia*". The concept is both very simple and very profound. Wisdom is *cognitio* because it is accessible to human faculties and rationally comprehensible.

The supreme truths of Religion are in Revelation, hence *notitia*. God communicates them, in a certain sense he reveals them. Then it is up to man to accept or reject them since free will is his supreme right and privilege.

The ostensory – or monstrance – with the consecrated host in the centre of the altar is the perspective and conceptual focus of the entire composition. In the upper part of the fresco, the three figures of the Holy Trinity are in line with the Eucharistic Host and visibly incarnate it. In the lower part of the fresco

there is a vast assembly of Doctors of the Church: Ambrose and Augustine, Jerome and Gregory in eminent positions, seated on thrones while all the others are standing or arranged in various ways. We can recognize Saint Bonaventure of Bagnoregio, Saint Thomas Aquinas, as well as Beato Angelico, Dante Alighieri, along with Girolamo Savonarola, who was burned in Florence not too many years before. Now, Julius II, a Franciscan wanted his image among the saints, out of hatred for Alexander VI, the Borgia pope and his predecessor who had wanted the monk put to death.

The fresco has always been called *Disputation of the Sacrament*. The responsibility for this totally inappropriate title lies with Giorgio Vasari who in his *Lives* had written about "disputing" figures. Actually, the saints and Doctors are not "disputing", but rather they are astounded and deeply stirred by the great mystery, and they seek the explanation of the sublime and inconceivable miracle of the Word Incarnate in their books.

The human mind is bewildered, consternated and feels totally inadequate when faced with the Truth revealed. Fortunately, we are helped by the merciful presence of God who sends His angel to support and console us. This is the meaning of the beautiful blond youth at the edge of the presbytery

where the theologians are gathered who, with sweetness and grace, invites us to adore the Eucharist.

The iconographic programme that unfolds on the walls of the Room of the Segnatura follows a logic that is as impeccable as it is fascinating. Man forces himself to rationally comprehend the reasons of things because that is his duty (*The School of Athens*). By exercising his free will, he accepts the Revelation (*Disputation of the Sacrament*). However, his existence on earth would not be complete, or even possible if it were not for the consolation of Beauty and the certainty of the Law.

The two short walls of the room celebrate Poetry and Law. On one side is the *Parnassus,* the mountain sacred to Phoebus Apollo, depicted here playing a *lira da braccio*, surrounded by the Muses and the great poets of all eras. The opposite wall is dedicated to Justice which, inspired by the Virtues, becomes real in history's greatest laws: Justinian's *Corpus Iuris Civilis* (also called the Pandects), and the *Decretals* of Gregory IX, an early pope portrayed with the face of Julius II.

Poetry is inspired by Divinity. In fact, the allegorical figure on the ceiling above Parnassus says "*Numine afflatur*". Poets exist because Phoebus Apollo plays his music, because they are touched by the spirit of the god. Both ancients and moderns render homage to the god of

A view of the Room of the Segnatura
with *Justice* and the *Disputation
of the Sacrament*

Beauty. Above, in a privileged position is the blind Homer, accompanied by Virgil and Dante. Sappho the poetess of love in the foreground, has Petrarch, her modern counterpart, to her left. And there are Boccaccio, Sannazzaro, Ariosto whom we can recognize in the group to right going up towards Parnassus. This is the group which, in the beginning and in the foreground, symmetrically with the image of Sappho points to an elderly poet laureate who may perhaps be Horace.

The other short wall is a glorification of the Law and of the Virtues that must inspire it. And here, in the lunette are the Cardinal Virtues (*Fortitude*, *Prudence* and *Temperance*) that potentially exist in each man, and the Theological Virtues (*Faith*, *Hope* and *Charity*) that come from God. Raphael depicted the Theological Virtues as youths: one (Faith) points to the sky with a finger; another (Hope) holds a burning torch; the third (Charity) is taking something from the branches of an oak – the heraldic symbol of the della Rovere pope, Julius II. The Cardinal Virtues, on the other hand, are women in various poses. Prudence looks behind herself through

a mirror held by a winged *putto*; Temperance shows us the reins needed to control the pace and hence, through a metaphor, the works and lives of men; Fortitude, strong and watchful, leans against the pope's oak tree. Justice, the fourth Cardinal Virtue, does not appear in this grouping because it is represented in the scroll-cartouche with the words "*unicuique suum*" and by the iconographic symbols – the scales and sword – on the corresponding portion of the ceiling.

The Emperor Justinian receiving the *Corpus Iuris Civilis* from Tribonian and Pope Gregory IX, who, portrayed with the features of Julius II, receives the *Decretals* are the protagonists of the history of law. Next to the Pope (the bearded figure) are two cardinals who would later become popes and play important roles in the history of the Church and of the arts: Giovanni de' Medici and Alessandro Farnese, the future Leo X and Paul III, respectively.

In addition to the allegorical figures arranged in relation to the various themes, Raphael's frescoes in the Room of the Segnatura, include four biblical and mythological scenes. *Phi-

losophy* above *The School of Athens*, is flanked by *The Prime Mover* symbolizing the origin of things. Next to *Poetry* is the *Flaying of Marsyas* – Apollo flayed Marsyas alive after he lost a contest to him. The *Judgement of Solomon* rivals *Justice*, and *Theology* is the counterpart to *Original Sin*.

A polychrome wainscot, simulating gilded bronze and framed by caryatids runs along all the walls in the room. This exquisite fresco decoration was painted in 1541 by Perin del Vaga, one of the most talented pupils to come out of Raphael's workshop.

If work on the frescoes in the Room of the Segnatura began late in the summer of 1508 starting from the wall with the *Disputation* (certainly the earliest part that is still reminiscent of a fifteenth century *mise en page,* with some residual nostalgia for Perunginesque symmetry and rhythm, and orderly Florentine beauty in the manner of Fra' Bartolomeo and Mariotto Albertinelli) it is reasonable to believe that by the end of 1511, Raphael had already opened the worksite in the adjacent room, that we know as the *Stanza di Eliodoro* – the Room of Heliodorus.

Raphael
The School of Athens (1509)
Room of the Segnatura

1. Plato (Leonardo da Vinci)
2. Aristotle
3. Socrates
4. Xenophon
5. Aeschines (or Alcibiades)
6. Alcibiades or (Alexander the Great)
7. Zeno
8. Epicurus
9. Federico Gonzaga
10. Averroes
11. Pythagoras
12. Francesco Maria della Rovere
13. Heraclitus (Michelangelo)
14. Diogenes
15. Euclid (Bramante)
16. Zoroaster (Pietro Bembo?)
17. Ptolemy
18. Raphael (self-portrait)

Raphael
Room of the Segnatura
The ceiling

Raphael
The Prime Mover
Room of the Segnatura
underside of the arch

Raphael
Philosophy
Room of the Segnatura
ceiling medallion

CAVSA
RVM

COGNI
TIO

Michelangelo and Raphael in the Vatican

Raphael
Averroes and Pythagoras

Detail of *The School of Athens* (1509),
Room of the Segnatura

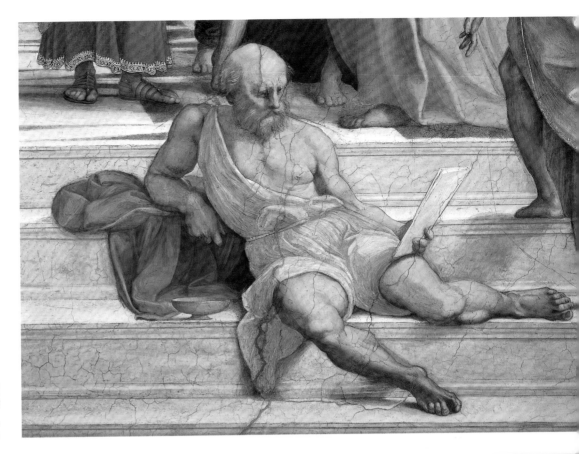

Raphael
Diogenes

Detail of *The School of Athens* (1509),
Room of the Segnatura

Raphael
Euclid

Detail of *The School of Athens* (1509),
Room of the Segnatura

Raphael
Plato and Aristotle
Detail of *The School of Athens* (1509),
Room of the Segnatura

Raphael
Heraclitus
Detail of *The School of Athens* (1509),
Room of the Segnatura
The Greek philosopher is a portrait of Michelangelo.

Raphael
Disputation of the Sacrament (1508-1509)
Room of the Segnatura

TOP

1. The Eternal Father
2. The Word Incarnate
3. Angels
4. The Virgin Mary
5. Saint John the Baptist

CENTRE

6. Saint Peter
7. Adam
8. Saint John the Evangelist
9. David
10. Saint Lawrence
11. Jeremiah (?)
12. Angels with the Gospels
13. The Holy Spirit
14. Judas Maccabeus (?)
15. Saint Stephen
16. Moses
17. Saint James the Lesser
18. Abraham
19. Saint Paul

BOTTOM

20. Beato Angelico
21. Bramante
22. Francesco Maria della Rovere
23. Gregory the Great (portrait of Julius II)
24. Saint Jerome
25. Saint Ambrose
26. Saint Augustine
27. Saint Thomas Aquinas
28. Innocent III
29. Saint Bonaventure
30. Sixtus IV
31. Dante
32. Girolamo Savonarola

Raphael
Saints and Doctors of the Church
Detail of *Disputation of the Sacrament*
(1508-1509),
Room of the Segnatura

In the group of Theologians, Gregory the Great
and Saint Jerome are to the left of the fresco.

Raphael
Theology

Room of the Segnatura,
ceiling medallion

Raphael
*The Holy Trinity, the Virgin Mary,
Saint John the Baptist and four angels
with the Gospels*

Detail of *Disputation of the Sacrament*
(1508–1509),
Room of the Segnatura

DIVINAR
RER

NOTI
TIA

SECUN
DUM MAT
LIBER
GENERA
TIONIS

INITIU
DU EVANGE
M MAR LII IESU
CUM CHRISTI

SECUN
DUM
LUCAM
FUIT
IN DIE
GIS

SEC IN PRIN
UND CIPIO ER
UM AT VERB
IOA UM ET VE
NN RBUM ER

Raphael
Parnassus (1510)
Room of the Segnatura

1. Apollo
2. Calliope
3. Terpsichore
4. Erato
5. Polymnia
6. Melpomene
7. Urania
8. Thalia
9. Clio
10. Euterpe
11. Statius
12. Virgil
13. Homer
14. Dante

15. Ennius
16. Anacreon
17. Petrarch
18. Corinna
19. Alcaeus
20. Sappho
21. Ariosto
22. Boccaccio
23. Tibullus
24. Tebaldeo
25. Propertius
26. Ovid
27. Sannazzaro
28. Horace

Raphael
Apollo among the Muses
Detail of *Parnassus* (1510),
Room of the Segnatura

Raphael
Conversation among poets:
Sappho and Petrarch
Detail of *Parnassus* (1510),
Room of the Segnatura

Raphael
Dante, Homer and Virgil
Detail of *Parnassus* (1510),
Room of the Segnatura

Raphael
Poetry
Room of the Segnatura,
ceiling medallion

Raphael
The wall of *Justice*
Room of the Segnatura

Raphael
***The Cardinal and Theological
Virtues*** (1510)
Room of the Segnatura

Raphael
Judgement of Solomon

Room of the Segnatura,
underside of the arch

Raphael
*Gregory IX (portrayed with the face
of Julius II) receives the Decretals
from Raimundo de Peñafort*

Detail of *Justice*
Room of the Segnatura

Raphael
Justice

Room of the Segnatura,
ceiling medallion

Room of Heliodorus

If the subject of the Room of the Segnatura is the destiny of man divided between Knowledge and Revelation, between Beauty and Law, the theme of the Audience Room (now called the "Room of Heliodorus") celebrates God's interventions in history defending the Church.

The Omnipotent banishes the sacrilegious Heliodorus from the Temple, liberates Saint Peter from Prison and stops Attila at the gates of Rome. The pope is the keeper of the *Corpus Christi*, and that is why he is shown in the scene of the miracle in *Mass at Bolsena* that occurred three centuries earlier. Devotion to the Cross, faith in the death and resurrection of Christ are the rock upon which the Church represented by Julius II rests, and that God will never abandon. Raphael related all this in the roughly two years (1512-1514) that he worked in the Room of Heliodorus assisted by the members of his workshop. The political message conveyed by the frescoes in this room of the papal apartment was extremely clear to his contemporaries and is also perfectly comprehensible to us, five centuries later. Julius II had made the defence of the autonomy and freedom of the Church the main,

if not exclusive, objective of his papacy. The Church could only exercise her spiritual authority (against heretics and schismatics, against simoniacs and corruptors of the ilk of Alexander VI, the Borgia pope) if she had strong and universally recognized temporal power.

This was Julius II's constant thought and to achieve this political aim he committed himself to ongoing wars against the Italian princes and the king of France. In the scenes in the Room of Heliodorus, the pope is portrayed with a beard: after losing Bologna, the second city in the Patrimony of Saint Peter in 1511, he had vowed not to shave until the French left Italian soil.

The iconographic themes of this room were a novelty for Raphael. For the first time he could test himself against history and depict heroic feats and miracles (the *Liberation of Saint Peter*, the *Mass at Bolsena*, the *Meeting between Leo the Great and Attila*), and could express himself in the "grand" manner that Michelangelo had just displayed on the ceiling of the Sistine Chapel that was officially unveiled on 31 October 1512. Raphael responded to this new and decisive challenge by changing his style. Thanks to his amazing versatility and his ability to absorb and transform any idea (these are the true distinctive features of his artistic personality), he was able to shift key – from the Segnatura to Heliodorus – in just a few months.

And he paid appropriate homage to Buonarroti. We can readily say that he embraced the new ways of depicting motion, anatomy and dramatic action with a graceful ductility. He adopted both the Mannerist vocabulary and syntax invented by Michelangelo to the point that in the mural with the *Expulsion of Heliodorus from the Temple*, the agitated and turbulent group of sacrilegious thieves trampled by the divine horseman (*2 Macc.* 3:23-29) seems to anticipate Giuliano Romano's frescoes in Palazzo Te in Mantua. The ceiling with the four Biblical scenes painted by the workshop to the master's drawings (*Moses and the Burning Bush*, the *Sacrifice of Isaac*, *Jacob's Dream*, *Noah Leaving the Ark*) is so filled with such precise citations of the Sistine Chapel that it was almost embarrassing (Vasari 1550). And yet (and this gives us the real measure of his greatness), Raphael did not feel guilty because he was not "copying" in the trivial and vulgar meaning of the word. He took abundantly from the immense repertoire of Nature and figures (from the masterpieces of classical antiquity, from Michelangelo, from Sebastiano del Piombo, from Lorenzo Lotto documented in the Palazzi Apostolici during that period, and in fact still present, on the ceiling of the Room of Heliodorus, with minor decorative frescoes, by Piero della Francesca whose famous mural was demolished to make room for the new decorations ordered by Julius II). He breathed Rome's heroic air and made it his own, and through that, he developed totally new concepts, solutions and styles.

In the frescoes in the Room of Heliodorus we can see his debts to Michelangelo, to Venetian colour propagated by Sebastiano del Piombo; we see attention to natural renderings of skin, to the physiognomical and psychological intensity of the Renaissance portrait as taught and exemplified by Lorenzo Lotto during those years.

All this and more contributed to "making" the Raphael of the Room of Heliodorus. The end result, however, is something that consumes and regenerates, it refreshes each concept from the immense figurative culture he assimilated and then developed. In this sense, the Raphael of the Room of Heliodorus is something totally new. This is an artist who was part of his day, and yet at the same time prefigured and anticipated artists and stylistic seasons yet to come.

Let us look at the famous scene with the *Liberation of Saint Peter*. The *Acts of the Apostles* (12:4-10) tell us that when Peter was imprisoned by Herod, an angel appeared in a dream and released him from his chains so that he could carry out his mission in Jerusalem.

The wall has a window, Raphael overcame this constraint by arranging the scene somewhat like a triptych and creating a light source for each "panel".

In the centre, the angel enters the prison cell. A blinding light reveals the black grate with a brilliant optical effect and transforms the two armed guards into steely, immobile mannequins that seem hypnotized by the miracle.

In the scene to the right, is a bewildered Saint Peter who has just left the prison. The light-bearing angel accompanies him leading the way. In that pale light amidst the darkness and wonder of the night, the soldiers overcome by sleep, fallen to the ground in the most diverse positions, take on unsettling forms and conjure up the surreal. To the left is the famous nocturnal scene dominated by the moon, a moon partially concealed by the clouds, high in the dull, sultry sky of a summer night that is sliding towards dawn at the gates of Rome.

In the universal history of painting, before Caravaggio, before Rembrandt's *Night Watch,* before the *Third of May* by Goya, there is the moonlit night that Raphael painted in 1512 (or 1513) in the Room of Heliodorus in the Vatican. At this point in his stylistic development Raphael was a brilliant architect and set-designer. We see him in the *Expulsion of Heliodorus from the Temple*. The interior space where the high priest Onias prays for the hand of the Almighty to stop the sacrilegious thief is an "almost pre-Baroque" invention

(Redig de Campos 1950) filled with dramatic tensions. And this Raphael, of the Room of Heliodorus was also a formidable portraitist. The bearded pope carried on his gestatorial chair in the foreground of the *Expulsion* is an unforgettable image and a dire warning to anyone who would sack and devastate the treasures of the Church.

In the scene of the *Mass at Bolsena*, more than by the cardinals (Raffaele Riario and Leonardo Grosso della Rovere) behind the pope participating in the historical commemoration of the miracle of Transubstantiation, we are impressed by the kneeling attendants in the right foreground. They are soldiers, German-speaking officers, fair-complexioned and blonde, proud of their gleaming armour and polychrome velvet and satin clothes. They fill the scene with their clearly commanding presence. At that time, no one in Italy would have been capable of expressing physiognomical and spiritual perspicuity in a male portrait with a resoluteness even vaguely comparable to what Raphael achieved here with sublime confidence and simplicity. If a comparison were possible, we would have to look at Albrecht Dürer's contemporary portraits.

The *Meeting between Leo the Great and Attila* is the last of the frescoes painted in the Room of Heliodorus. The episode it portrays is very old and mixes history with legend. Attila invaded It-

Raphael
The Room of Heliodorus

with the *Mass at Bolsena* (1512), on the left
and the *Meeting between Leo the Great
and Attila* (1512-1513), on the right.

aly in 452 and was heading for Rome.
Pope Leo went to meet him at the Min-
cio River near Mantua and persuaded
him to turn back and thereby saved
Rome from destruction.

Legend has it that Attila and his gener-
als decided to renounce the conquest of
Rome not so much – or only because
of the Pope's words, but because they
saw the armed figures of the Saints Peter and Paul appear in the sky. Julius II
conceived of the fresco as both a po-

litical manifesto (the Holy See's firm
opposition to the foreign presence in
Italy), and as an ex voto, out of gratitude: the French decided to leave the
peninsula in June 1512.

Julius II died on 21 February 1513 and
Cardinal Giovanni de' Medici, the son
of Lorenzo the Magnificent ascended
to the throne of Saint Peter as Pope
Leo X. As everyone knows, the Medici
pope was a consummate intellectual
and discriminating connoisseur of the

arts. He admired Raphael without res-
ervations, and was his intelligent and
well as generous patron. His years of
glory unfolded in parallel with those
of the artist and practically coincided
in time. In fact, he died one year after
Raphael, in 1521. This explains why,
starting from the scene of the encoun-
ter with Attila, the pope's face is portrayed in the historical images frescoed
in all the Stanze and in the Room of
Leo X.

Raphael
Mass at Bolsena (1512)
Room of Heliodorus

Raphael's workshop was becoming more and more prominent. His pupils, men of twenty whom the documents describe as *giovani* – youths, or *garzoni* – boys, were capable of setting up a worksite, managing it and completing the project. They were Giulio Romano, Giovan Francesco Penni (both of whom played leading roles) along with Perin del Vaga, Polidoro da Caravaggio, Giovanni da Udine, and Pellegrino da Modena. We have to imagine the master who, with his "effortless" creativity and amazing ability to persuade and charm that everyone acknowledged, not only provided ideas, sketches and cartoons, but gave advice, intervened and corrected in a dialogue with colleagues who were only slightly younger than himself.

The presence of the workshop "team", and in this case particularly of Giovan Francesco Penni, is evident in the *Meeting between Leo the Great and Attila*. In the mural, Raphael's hand must be limited to the left side depicting the papal retinue and the formidable landscapes in the background: Monte Mario ablaze with fires and the spectral outlines of the Colosseum and aqueducts. The right side with the mass of horses and riders crowding around Attila is mainly the work of Penni who, using the master's ideas and drawings, created a true masterpiece of thrilling vitality and wild energy.

Raphael
Pope Julius II
Detail of the *Mass at Bolsena* (1512)
Room of Heliodorus

Raphael
The Pope's Chair-bearers
Detail of the *Mass at Bolsena* (1512)
Room of Heliodorus

Raphael
Expulsion of Heliodorus from the Temple (1511)

Room of Heliodorus

1. The Divine Messenger
2. Heliodorus
3. The High Priest Onias
4. Pope Julius II
5. Giulio Romano (portrait of Raphael?)
6. Marcantonio Raimondi
7. Gian Pietro dei Foliari

Raphael and helpers
The ceiling in the Room of Heliodorus

X · ANN · D · M · D · X · IIII

Raphael
Liberation of Saint Peter (1511-1512)
and detail
Room of Heliodorus

This famous nocturnal scene is dominated
by the moon, a moon partially concealed
by clouds, high in the dull, sultry sky
of a summer night and sliding towards dawn
at the gates of Rome.

Michelangelo and Raphael in the Vatican

Raphael,
Giovan Francesco Penni and helpers
Meeting between Leo the Great and Attila (1513)
Room of Heliodorus

1. Pope Leo X
2. Cardinal Giovanni de' Medici (the future Pope Leo X)
3. Paris de' Grassi, papal Master of Ceremonies
4. Giovanni Lazzaro de' Magistris (called Serapica), chamberlain to the pope
5. Saint Peter
6. Saint Paul
7. The Colosseum
8. Attila

on the following pages:

Raphael,
Giovan Francesco Penni and helpers
Meeting between Leo the Great and Attila (1513)
Room of Heliodorus

details
Saints Peter and Paul;
Horses and Huns, to the left;
Leo the Great (with the face of Pope Leo X),
Cardinals Alfonso Petrucci (?)
and Sigismondo Gonzaga,
master of ceremonies Paris de' Grassis
and Serapica, to the right.

The Vatican Rooms

Room
of the *Fire in Borgo*

In documents, the room we know as the "dell'Incendio di Borgo" is described as the "*triclinium*", a dining room for receiving just a few persons. The frescoes, painted between 1514 and 1517, celebrate the feats of early popes called Leo, and they are all portrayed with the face of the Medici pope. There is Leo III crowning Charlemagne "Holy Roman Emperor" on Christmas night in the year 800 (it is important to note that the emperor is depicted with the face of Francis I signifying the refound friendship between the Holy See and the French Crown) and taking his oath in Saint Peter's.

And there is Leo IV, putting out the fire that was devastating the Borgo district with the sign of the cross and defeating the Saracen pirates at the mouth of the Tiber in the *Battle of Ostia*.

The four scenes are crowned by a ceiling decorated a few years earlier by Pietro Perugino with grotesques, leaves and antique cameos forming four tondos, in the centre of each vaulting cell, which allow us to understand the room's original purpose, when Julius II used it as the seat of the highest ecclesiastical court, *Signatura*

Gratiae et Iustitiae. The Perugino tondos depict *Christ between Mercy and Justice, Christ as the Sol Iustitiae*, the *Holy Trinity and the Twelve Apostles*, and the *Creator Enthroned with Angels and Cherubs*.

When Raphael began work in this room he decided not to do anything with the ceiling, and according to Vasari it was out of respect for his former teacher. The hypothesis is plausible, as in the case of Sodoma's paintings that were left intact on the ceiling of the Room of the Segnatura: once again Raphael confirmed his kindness of spirit and ability to charm and seduce that fascinated his contemporaries.

The master himself probably did very little painting in the Room of the *Fire in Borgo*. And yet, his creations would be destined to multiply and make the history of art bear exquisite fruits in Italy and throughout Europe. The wall frescoed with the *Fire* is justifiably famous. It was fundamental to all the classicists, from Guido Reni to Poussin to David. The female figures in the foreground, the woman with her arms raised to the sky and the other, seen from the rear with the amphora on her head, the terrorized nude climbing down from the wall, Aeneas carrying his father Anchises on his back leaving a Troy that was reinvented and placed next to the early Constantinian Basilica of Saint Peter, are true arche-

types of modern painting. They have been copied by countless engravers, and cited and interpreted by generations of artists.

The frescoes in the Room of the *Fire in Borgo* convey a political message of pacification and re-established international order. Times changed after the reign of Julius II that had been marked by years of harsh diplomatic and military clashes between the papacy and the French Crown. In October 1515, the king signed the concordat with the Church and the Medici pope trusting in a future of amicable relations.

It is for this reason that in the *Coronation of Charlemagne* the emperor has the face of Francis I and the scroll on the right edge of the frame says that Charlemagne and by extension all of France, are the sword and shield of the Church ("*Carolus Magnus Ro[manae] Ecclesiae ensis clypeusque*").

The scene with the *Oath of Leo III*, depicting an episode that took place the day before the coronation, also brims political-religious meanings. In fact, the *Liber Pontificalis* says that on the eve of Charlemagne's consecration as emperor, Leo III wanted to clear himself before the sovereign and the clergy of the calumnious charges that had been brought against him.

"*Dei non hominum est episcopos iudicare*" – It is up to God and not men

Pietro Perugino
Christ between Mercy and Justice
Room of the *Fire in Borgo*,
ceiling medallion,
Christ depicted between the Baptist and
Satan who is disguised as an old man.

to judge the bishops – is inscribed in the mock scroll painted on the frame. This proud affirmation of the Church's total autonomy with regard to the secular powers emerged during the eleventh session of the Lateran Council (19 December 1516) and as we would say now, it appeared in the pope's dining room "in real time".

The *Battle of Ostia* also refers to a distant episode: the Saracens attacked at the mouth of the Tiber and were repulsed in 849, during the reign of Leo IV. Together with Cardinal Giulio de' Medici – who would become Pope Clement VII – and Cardinal Bernardo Dovizi da Bibbiena, the Medici pope looks on proudly and happily as the Christian forces win the battle and take prisoners while the naval battle continues to rage in the water. The choice of this iconographic subject is explained by Leo X's interest in the "crusade", the utopistic objective that was never achieved by the Renaissance popes.

Images of some of history's most famous Christian princes – Godfrey of Bouillon, Aistulf, Ferdinand the Catholic, Lothair, Charlemagne and Constantine – are depicted in the monochrome wainscoting that runs along all four walls completing the iconographic theme of the primacy of the Pope of Rome and the alliance between the Throne and the Altar.

Raphael and helpers
Fire in Borgo (1514-1517*)*
Room of the *Fire in Borgo*

and detail
A group of women and children
frightened by the fire.

Raphael and helpers
Fire in Borgo (1514-1517*)*
Room of the *Fire in Borgo*

and details
Aeneas carrying his father, Anchises, on his back;
the young Ascanius; women carrying water.

Raphael and helpers
Coronation of Charlemagne (1514-1517)
Room of the *Fire in Borgo*

Charlemagne, sword and shield of the Church of Rome
and detail of the wainscoting.

Raphael and helpers
Coronation of Charlemagne (1514-1517)
Room of the *Fire in Borgo*

Leo III (with the face of Leo X)
crowns Charlemagne (a portrait of Francis I).

Raphael and helpers
Oath of Leo III (1514-1517)
Room of the *Fire in Borgo*

and detail
Leo III (with the features of Leo X) takes the oath
in Saint Peter's Basilica;

on the altar frontal, the *Martyrdom of Saint Catherine
of Alexandria.*

The Vatican Rooms

Raphael and helpers
Battle of Ostia (1514-1517)
Room of the *Fire in Borgo*

and detail
Leo IV (with the face of Leo X) witnesses the victory
of the Christian armies and the taking of prisoners.

Room of Constantine

The itinerary of Raphael's Rooms in the Vatican Museums concludes with the Sala di Costantino (Room of Constantine). It is a very big room and highly suited to prestigious ceremonies. It was conceived for this type of function by the Medici popes, Leo X and Clement VII who commissioned the painted decorations. Walking into the Room of Constantine we see frescoes that seem like tapestries, depicting the historical triumphs of the Catholic Church. Constantine guided by the vision of the Cross defeats his enemy Maxentius, is baptized by Pope Sylvester and gives Rome to the Pope.

Leo X commissioned Raphael to design the decorations, and according to his personal friend and biographer, Paolo Giovio, the artist began work in the spring of 1519. Raphael died the following year and the assignment went to Giulio Romano and Giovan Francesco Penni since they had the drawings and plans.

By the time Leo X died in 1521, the room was more than half finished. After an interruption during the reign of Hadrian VI (1522-1523), the work was resumed at full pace when another Medici pope, the learned patron of the arts, Clement VII ascended to Peter's throne. The entire fresco cycle was completed in the summer of 1525: the main scenes of the *Vision of the Cross*, the *Battle of the Milvian Bridge*, the *Baptism of Constantine*, and the *Donation of Rome*, portraits of the popes flanked by allegories of the Virtues, and monochrome renderings of countless episodes of religious and secular history that run in an uninterrupted band on the wainscot along the walls.

We know that Raphael prepared the iconographic programme for the entire room (the frescoes on the ceiling and the lunettes with the *Triumph of the Christian Religion* and the allegorical portrayals of the provinces of Italy were painted much later, between 1582 and 1585) and that he did the drawings of the *Allocution* and the *Battle*. His pupils transposed the drawings into painting, and one of them played a dominant role: Giulio Pippi, called Giulio Romano, who was the most talented of all.

This "meeting" between Raphael's genius and Giulio's inspired talent made the wall that hosts the two scenes one of the greatest and most fascinating painted masterpieces of the Italian Renaissance. And there is one rightly famous detail that justifies this statement: the *Battle of the Milvian Bridge* with Maxentius drowning in the Tiber overwhelmed by Constantine's victorious cavalry. Only Rubens, a century later, would be able to attain this prodigious level of depicting Truth, evoking History, and portraying Life with all its passions and glories.

The Room of Constantine presented Raphael's last and greatest stylistic achievement to the world of art in the mid-1520's, shortly before the Sack of Rome (1527).

FRVCTIFICVS ARBORE PIGENS

FRVMENTO LETVS VPPIVS

HETRVSCA DISCIPLINA

VICTOR GENTIV ROMANVS

Michelangelo and Raphael in the Vatican

Tommaso Laureti
Triumph of the Christian Religion (1582-1585)
Room of Constantine,
detail of the ceiling

The triumph of Christianity over paganism,
painted by Sebastiano del Piombo's disciple
by order of Gregory XIII and Sixtus V.

A view of the Room of Constantine (1519-1525)
with the *Battle of the Milvian Bridge* to the left
and the *Baptism of Constantine* to the right.

The Vatican Rooms

Within the fresco, the following inscriptions appear:

ANNO DNI
MDLXXXV

AVG·ET

C·VAL·AV
IMP·VICT
MAXENT
OPES

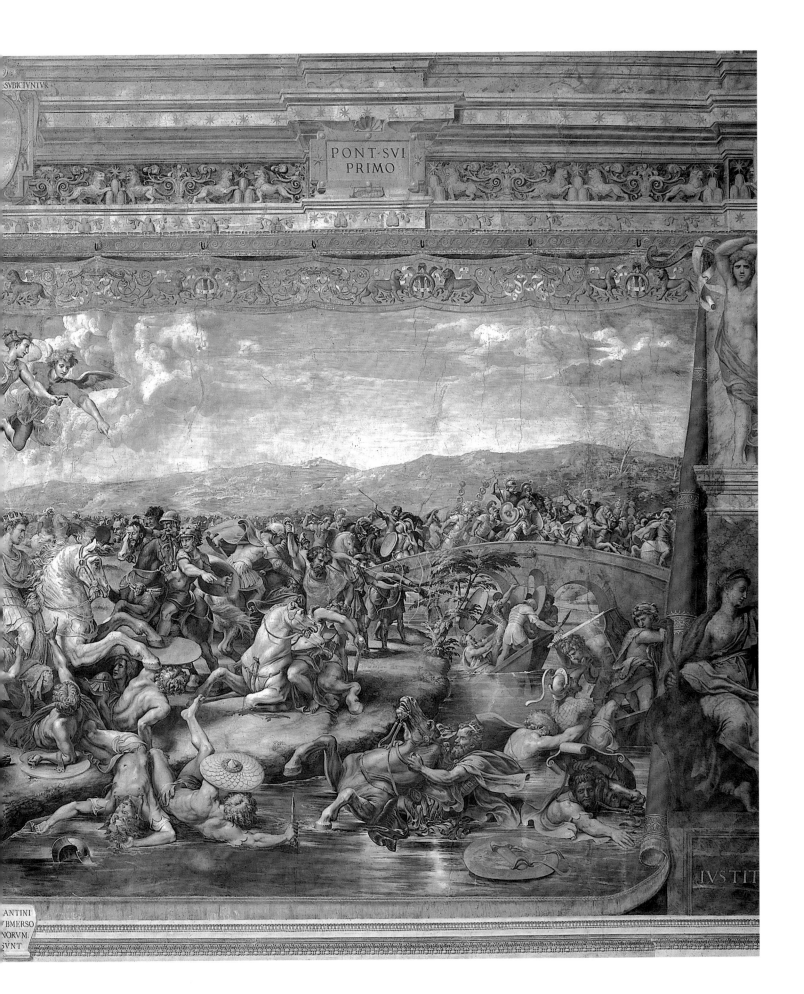

on the preceding pages:
School of Raphael, Giulio Romano,
Giovan Francesco Penni and helpers
Battle of the Milvian Bridge (1519-1525)
Room of Constantine

School of Raphael, Giulio Romano,
Giovan Francesco Penni and helpers
Baptism of Constantine (1519-1525)
Room of Constantine

School of Raphael, Giulio Romano,
Giovan Francesco Penni and helpers
Donation of Rome (1519-1525)
Room of Constantine

School of Raphael, Giulio Romano,
Giovan Francesco Penni and helpers
Vision of the Cross (1519-1525)
Room of Constantine

The inscription in the beam of light
at the top reads: «In this sign you will conquer».

and detail
Clement I

The Vatican Loggias

View of Raphael's Loggias (1518-1519)
Vatican City, Palazzo Apostolico

Raphael, who took over from Bramante as works director, completed the loggia in 1519. The Second Loggia, on the same floor as the apartment used by Julius II and Leo X, was the first to be decorated by Raphael and his school (painters, stucco workers and masons). Taking his inspiration from classical art, Raphael brought the "grotesques" into fashion (the name comes from the decorations in the recently discovered *Domus Aurea* of Nero, called "grottoes" because they were underground) and they were used to decorate countless palaces. Leo X placed his personal art collection in this loggia, called "Raphael's".

We cannot leave the Raphael of the Rooms without a few words about the Loggias. Without mentioning the covered gallery with its thirteen spans in the middle of the triple portico created by Donato Bramante to camouflage the old Palazzo Apostolico and connect it to the Belvedere that Raphael and his team decorated during the final years of the 1510s.

The Loggias are not part of the museum itinerary. In fact, they are inside the area of the Vatican that hosts offices of the Government and the Secretary of State. Permission has to be requested to see them; it is usually granted quite readily for reasons of study.

There was a time that people came to the Vatican to see the classical statues, the *Laocoön,* the *Belvedere Apollo,* the *Ariadne* and even more for Raphael, the Raphael of the Rooms and the Loggias. It was not like today when people come for Michelangelo who was considered too dramatic, too brutal, too everything. Things change with the passing of generations: tastes change and so do the aesthetic ideals of men and women.

We have to consider the enormous success that Raphael's Loggias enjoyed in Europe between the sixteenth and nineteenth centuries. Their example influenced the development of art from France to Germany; generations of artists considered them the supreme model for inspiration. For intellectuals and for Europe's royal courts they were "the taste" and "the style" without any need for further explanations or specifications.

To understand what Raphael's Loggias meant for the world's culture we must go to the Hermitage in Saint Petersburg. As everyone knows, the Hermitage is an immense, "omnivorous", almost excessive museum. All, or nearly all of Europe's and the world's figurative cultures are represented there. We walk for miles, along endless galleries and lavish rooms crowded with Roman and Renaissance statues, and paintings by Rembrandt, Rubens, and Titian.

In the Hermitage there is Greco-Roman, Middle Eastern and Asian archaeology; there are astounding ethnographic collections, there are the Impressionists, there are endless collections of weapons, furniture, tapestries, jewellery and *objets d'art.* The Hermitage leaves an indelible memory because it represents the voracity and the insatiable hunger the Russian tsars had for the figurative cultures of Europe and the world.

And yet, at a certain point along the itinerary, the inexperienced visitor who walks into the Hermitage for the first time will feel bewildered. Because not far from the room that hosts Antonio Canova's greatest masterpieces – *Hebe,* the *Three Graces, Cupid and Psyche* – he or she will come upon a space that is totally unexpected and unforeseeable. For an instant he will think that he is in Rome, in the Vatican,

Raphael and workshop
Last Supper (1518-1519)
Second Loggia

Raphael and workshop
**Moses Shows the Tablets of the Law
to the People of Israel**
(1518-1519)
Second Loggia

on the following pages:
Raphael and workshop
The ceilings of the first span (left)
and eighth span (right)
In the span are scenes from the *Creation* (clockwise
from the top): Creation of the sun and moon; God
separates the earth from the waters; God separates
light from darkness; creation of the animals.
In the eighth span *Scenes of Moses* (clockwise from
the top): Moses leads the people of Israel to safety
while the waters close over the Pharaoh's army, Moses
approaches the burning bush and is ordered to return
to Egypt to free the Jews, Moses saved from the waters,
Moses and the water springing from the rock.

and yet, he is five thousand kilometres from Rome, in the northerly light of the Gulf of Finland. It was, Catherine II – Catherine the Great – who wanted a clone of the Vatican Loggias in the capital of her immense and still semi-barbarian empire. She had never been to Rome. She only knew the Loggias from prints engraved by Giovanni Volpato but for her it was love at first sight. And so, the Italian architect Giacomo Quarenghi designed and built an exact, full-scale replica of the Vatican Loggias in the Hermitage and did so in record time, while back in Rome, Cristoforo Unterperger heading a large group of artists (Felice Giani, Giovan Battista Dell'Era, Wenzel Peter among others) supervised the copying. The eighteenth century was drawing to a close, Goethe who was in Rome in 1787 was just in time to see the copies that were ready to be shipped to Saint Petersburg: the paint was still wet and he spoke of them admiringly.

This episode, with Catherine the Great as the key player, is just one of the many possible examples we can mention of the huge success that Raphael's final fresco project had attained throughout the world.

Originally, the Loggias were open to the sky and Rome's landscape. The windows were only installed in the nineteenth century to protect paintings and stuccoes from otherwise unstoppable deterioration. On the ceiling, there is a sequence of fifty-two religious scenes. They are known as *Raphael's Bible,* a rendering in pictures of the best known and most popular scripture passages in the world. They have been reproduced countless times, from the sixteenth century engravings to the modern little holy pictures given to first communicants. All around, in the frescoes and the stuccoes that fill the walls, the glory of Antiquity – an endless repertoire of grotesques and relief images taken from classical statuary, carved gems, coins and medals – mix with the glories of Nature symbolized by a triumph of flowers, fruits and birds: the magnificent still-lifes by Giovanni da Udine. It is Nero's *Domus Aurea,* it is the splendour of visible beauty, all sanctified by Christian revelation.

What is most amazing is the speed with which it was designed and executed. On 16 June 1519 Baldassar Castiglione informed Isabella d'Este that the work was finished with these words: "And now he has a loggia that is painted and decorated with stuccoes, in the ancient manner, the work of Raphael, as beautiful as possible and perhaps even more [beautiful] that anything we can see today by the modern [painters]".

Raphael had less than one year to live. In the summer of 1519 he delivered the supreme masterpiece to his most discriminating and refined sovereign, the Medici pope, Leo X.

How could Raphael have produced such an enormous and demanding oeuvre in such a short time? This is the crucial question that every art historian has asked, and it also another proof of Raphael's great genius.

Like a film director, in the Loggias, Raphael provided the concept, defined the project, produced the drawings, watched over, controlled, suggested, corrected and then let the actors – the young men of his workshop – speak: Giulio Romano, Perin del Vaga, Polidoro da Caravaggio, Giovan Francesco Penni, Giovanni da Udine, Vincenzo Tamagni, the Frenchman Guillaume de Marcillat, and the artists from Spain, Pedro Machuca and Alonso Berruguete. Identifying the hand of each one, distinguishing the stylistic tendencies and variations of each helper is one of the most delicate and fascinating tasks in art-historical philology. It is an undertaking that has involved generations of scholars from the days of Giorgio Vasari to the recent monumental work by Nicole Dacos (2008).

However, there is one thing everyone agrees to, and that Baldassar Castiglione had grasped perfectly: thanks to Raphael's consolidating genius, the Loggias are the supreme achievement of "modern" art from the period that the manuals call "the Renaissance".

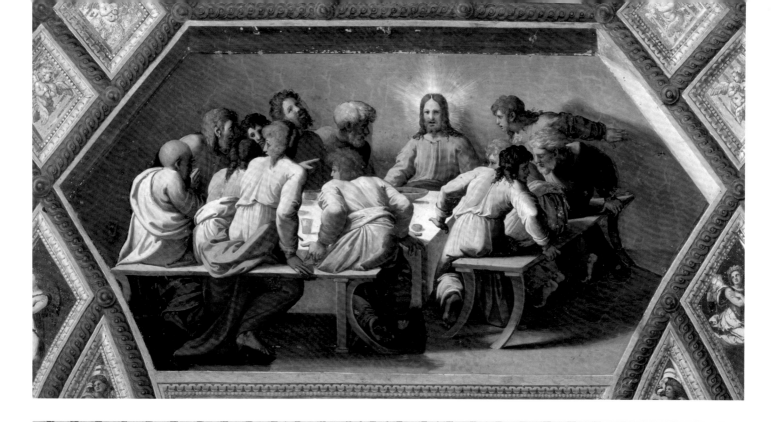

The Tapestries

The Vatican Museums have superb collections of tapestries which are on public display under the necessary conditions of reduced light and controlled temperature and humidity. But those who want to see the most beautiful tapestries in the world, must go to Room VIII of the Pinacoteca where the so-called Raphael Tapestries are on display, Raphael's cartoons (in the Victoria and Albert Museum, London) were commissioned by Pope Leo X and prepared between 1515 and 1516.

In 1517, in Brussels, the workshop of Pieter van Aelst, owner of the most famous factory in Europe, began transposing the cartoons into cloth. The entire series was destined for the Sistine Chapel. We can imagine the day, the Feast of Saint Stephen in 1519 when, as the chronicles tell us "the pontifical mass was held in the customary chapel [...] and that same day the pope ordered that his new and splendid and precious tapestries be hung, all deemed them to be more beautiful than any other thing on earth, they triggered the greatest admiration among all those who were present".

"*Sunt rebus quibus non est aliquid in orbe pulchrius…*" in these, the original Latin words of the chronicle written by the master of ceremonies Paris de Gras-

sis, we can grasp the amazement and admiration even more.

In fact, up to that day in 1519, not only had no one ever seen, no one had ever imagined anything as beautiful or as radically new. It was not merely a question of technical excellence and skill, of the exquisite crafting, of the luxury and extreme costs of the borders with the Medici coat of arms woven in gold thread and the sequences of sacred and profane scenes. What was striking then, and still fascinates us today, is the ability to mimic painting in fabric, and to even surpass it in portraying reality.

The nets make the waters of the lake tremble and ripple in *The Miraculous Draught of Fishes* and the feathery necks of the aquatic birds seem to throb – as they, too, witness the miracle.

In the *Handing over of the Keys* each rustle of the distant trees, every strip of cloud in the sky are portrayed, like the fleece of the sheep, like the colours of the meadows that stretch towards the horizon. The Flemish weavers were known for their outstanding technical skills, but the idea of including the infinite beauties of the world in the great story came from Raphael. It was the idea that Annibale Carracci and Domenichino, Pietro da Cortona and

Poussin would make their own one hundred years later.

Tragedy and pathos, emotion, glory and drama are all part of the tapestries so that each piece in the series becomes unforgettable. The *Stoning of Saint Stephen* is a tumultuous explosion of beastly violence that takes places against a vast, peaceful landscape of forests caressed by light, and of the majestic, distant outlines of the city. The *Saint Paul Preaching in Athens* is solemnity and majesty raised over the horrors of the world, almost a *School of Athens* replicated on a loom. While the *Conversion of Saint Paul* is the world's only depiction of the episode that has been able to compete with Michelangelo in the Pauline Chapel.

The scenes that Raphael's atelier put on paper, and the Brussels weavers translated into tapestries are taken from the *Acts of the Apostles*. Raphael designed and Pieter van Aelst created ten huge (nearly 4 metres long and more than 5 wide) depicting the following episodes: *The Miraculous Draught of Fishes*, the *Handing over of the Keys*, the *Healing of the Lame Man*, the *Death of Ananias*, the *Stoning of Saint Stephen*, the *Conversion of Saint Paul*, the *Blinding of Elymas*, the *Sacrifice at Lystra*, *Saint Paul Preaching in Athens*, and *Saint Paul in Prison*.

Anyone who is familiar with the *Acts of the Apostles* and the history of art is au-

on page 220:
View of the Sistine Chapel
with the tapestries made by the workshop
of Pieter van Aelst based on cartoons by Raphael.

Workshop of Pieter van Aelst,
based on cartoons by Raphael
the *Stoning of Saint Stephen* (1515-1519)
Vatican Museums, Pinacoteca

Workshop of Pieter van Aelst,
based on cartoons by Raphael
The Miraculous Draught of Fishes
(1515-1519)
Vatican Museums, Pinacoteca

tomatically and almost unconsciously drawn to visualizing the episodes of that book through Raphael's tapestries. This is precisely what happens when we look at the ceiling of the Loggia and see *Raphael's Bible*. For the art historian, for the scholar, for the intellectual as for ordinary Christians, this is the Bible, and there is no other. We cannot say it too often: it is precisely here, in that exquisite ability to make images from sacred and secular history (from the *Conversion of Saint Paul* to *Constantine's Allocution*) popular, definitive and eternal that Raphael's greatness lies.

We can try to imagine Raphael and his pope, Leo X, on 26 December, the Feast of Saint Stephen in 1519. We can imagine the astonishment and pride that both must have felt looking at the wonders of those cloths hung in the Sistine Chapel in the correct iconographic-scriptural order. To the right, beneath the scenes from the life of Christ, the story of Peter the Vicar; to the left, beneath the scenes of Moses, the scenes of Paul, Apostle of the Church "*ex gentibus*". And the series was not complete. Three more tapestries arrived in the Vatican some time later, before the end of 1521, the year that Leo X died, following Raphael who had left this world in 1520.

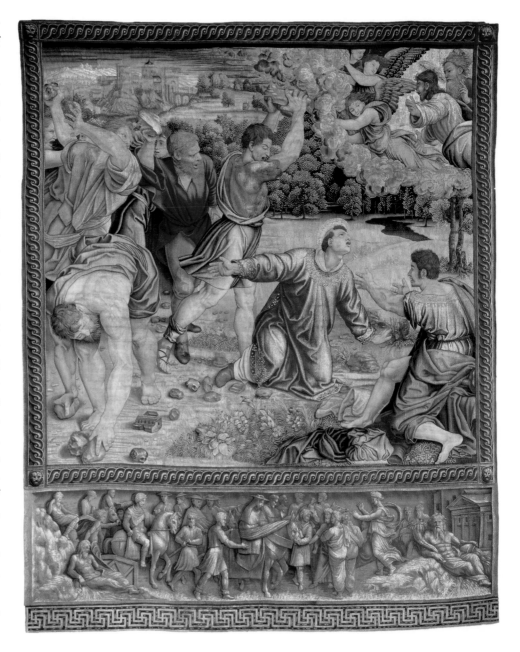

Workshop of Pieter van Aelst,
based on cartoons by Raphael
Handing over of the Keys (1515-1519)
Vatican Museums, Pinacoteca

Workshop of Pieter van Aelst,
based on cartoons by Raphael
Saint Paul Preaching in Athens
(1515-1519)
Vatican Museums, Pinacoteca

Workshop of Pieter van Aelst,
based on cartoons by Raphael
Conversion of Saint Paul (1515-1519)

Vatican Museums, Pinacoteca

Many years later (1542-1545), Michelangelo
painted a dramatic *Conversion* for Pope Paul III
in the Pauline Chapel.

The Paintings in the Pinacoteca Vaticana

Along with the tapestries, Room VIII, the heart of the Pinacoteca, also hosts Raphael's painted masterpieces: the *Oddi Altarpiece*, the predella with monochrome depictions of the *Theological Virtues*, the altarpiece called the *Madonna of Foligno* and the most famous of all, the *Transfiguration*. The way the museum is currently arranged, the paintings offer the visitor a concise look at three chronological and stylistic periods in Raphael's career. The *Oddi Altarpiece* (that gets its name because Maddalena Oddi commissioned it for the family chapel in the church of San Francesco al Prato in Perugia) is clearly from the artist's Peruginesque period (1502-1503), just before the sojourn in Florence that allowed Raphael to discover and embrace the great "modern style" of Fra' Bartolomeo, Leonardo, and Michelangelo. We can see Pietro Perugino's influence in this religious scene that centres on the *Coronation of the Virgin as Queen of Heaven*. We can understand this even better in the predella where the scenes with the *Annunciation*, the *Adoration of the Magi*, and the *Presentation in the Temple* are characterized by a melodious, rhythmic elegance. Looking at the *Oddi Altarpiece* we can understand that Raphael learned the secret of the rhythm that governs form and beauty, that makes them touch the heart and transfigures them from his teacher Perugino, and he never forgot that lesson.

In the monochrome predella with the three Theological Virtues flanked by winged *putti* (it was destined for the altarpiece commissioned by Atalanta Baglioni for the chapel of San Francesco al Prato in Perugia) the stylistic evolution that would lead to the Room of the Segnatura was already complete. The year was 1507, Raphael was twenty-four years old and he had already attained a full mastery domination of harmonious and classically monumental form, even in these small panels (18 x 44 cm).

The *Madonna of Foligno*, painted between 1511 and 1513, has had a difficult history. The worldly protagonist of the altarpiece is Sigismondo Conti, the prelate to the right, with his hands clasped, whom Saint Jerome presents to the Virgin Mary. This sacred portrayal has the meaning of an ex voto. The donor, together with the heavenly figures (the Virgin and Child up high in heaven in a glory of angels against the disk of the sun, and Saints Jerome, Francis and John the Baptist in the foreground) witness the miracle in the background: a meteorite had fallen on his house and left him unharmed.

The altarpiece was originally painted on wood. After the Peace of Tolentino (1791) the French took it Paris as war booty along with all the other Raphael paintings that are now in the Pinacoteca, and had it transferred to canvas. Sigismondo Conti belonged to an

Raphael
Madonna of Foligno
(1511-1513), detail
Vatican Museums, Pinacoteca

old Foligno family, when he died the painting was placed in the church of Santa Maria in Ara Coeli, Rome and from there it was moved to the convent called "delle contesse" at Foligno, hence the title, *Madonna of Foligno*. Antonio Canova brought the painting back to the Vatican in 1816.

To grasp Raphael's interest in colour in 1511-13 when he was working in the Room of Heliodorus, it is sufficient to stop and look at the landscape in the background of the altarpiece, it is a landscape so rich in colours and "tones", so sparkling and almost swarming with luminous matter that we immediately think (and it has also been written) of Dosso, of Lotto, and of Giorgione's "violet ashes".

The absolute masterpiece in Room VIII of the Pinacoteca is the *Transfiguration*. Although Cardinal Giulio de' Medici, later Pope Clement VII, commissioned it for the cathedral in Narbonne, was it placed in San Pietro in Montorio in Rome. It was taken away by Napoleon's troops and was returned to the Vatican in 1816. Here is the basic information about the painting that was part of the final days of the artist's life.

Vasari says that Raphael left the painting unfinished, the last brushstrokes were on the "countenance of Christ". Then he fell ill and died on 6 April 1520. The funeral was held in the Pantheon where Raphael still lies today in a marble sarcophagus for which his friend the poet Francesco Bembo wrote two memorable lines in Latin: "*magna parens frugum timuit quo sospite vinci et moriente mori*" – Nature feared that she would be subdued when he was alive and would die now that he is dead. With their elegance and splendour, these beautiful lines sum up the destiny of a painter who – as his contemporaries believed and we continue to believe – was the greatest of all times.

All of Rome mourned at the Pantheon that day, also because according to Vasari, the *Transfiguration* was placed behind Raphael's lifeless body, so that when they saw "that living picture in contrast with the dead body"[9], no one could hold back their tears.

In fact, the *Transfiguration* is the zenithal piece, the masterpiece of masterpieces, the painting that is at the acme of Raphael's entire output, concluding and exalting it from the spiritual and the stylistic standpoints.

The holy image is divided into two scenes. Below is the boy possessed by demons in the crowd of men and women around him, above is the transfigured Christ between Moses and Elijah. The lower part of the painting is filled with the drama of each and everyone, with fear, with embattled hope. Like every living being under the heavens, the boy possessed by evil asks to be liberated from the misfortune that is oppressing and devastating him. Those near him, his mother and the other figures want to help, they know that his salvation is also their own. But only Christ can save, as indicated by the Evangelist to the left with his hand stretched out pointing to the Transfigured Christ on Mount Tabor.

Dark, dramatically realistic, almost Caravaggesque tones, the effects of impassioned painting "in black" characterize the lower part of the composition, while above it is light that triumphs. Light is the word of Christ the Saviour and it is for this reason that His face shines like the noonday sun.

We stand in front of this painting and understand the essential. We understand the essence of Raphael like a mirror that reflects the world of God and the world of men. There is everything in Raphael's works, and in this sublime painting there is more than in any of the others. There are human passions, fears, conflicting sentiments (the group of agitated men and women in the foreground), there is the infinite splendour of the visible world (the Roman sunset behind Mount Tabor) there is the consolation of beauty that warms the heart and, at least for a moment, makes us happy that we are alive and have eyes to see.

Raphael
Madonna of Foligno
(1511-1513),
Vatican Museums, Pinacoteca
and details
The painting was first in the church
of Santa Maria in Ara Coeli in Rome,
then it was taken to the convent
of Sant'Anna called "delle Contesse"
in Foligno. Raphael painted the
altarpiece for Sigismondo de' Conti,
who had survived a meteorite that
had struck his house at Foligno
(the scene in the background).
At the right, the kneeling donor,
is presented to the Virgin by Saint
Jerome who places a hand on his
head, as Saint John the Baptist
and Saint Francis look on at the left.

Raphael
Oddi Altarpiece.
Coronation of the Virgin
(1502-1503),
Vatican Museums, Pinacoteca

The artist was not yet twenty years old,
and still clearly influenced by Perugino,
when he painted the altarpiece Maddalena
Oddi had commissioned it for the family
chapel in the church of San Francesco
al Prato in Perugia.

Raphael
Oddi Altarpiece.
Coronation of the Virgin
(1502-1503),
Vatican Museums, Pinacoteca

Predella panels
Annunciation
Adoration of the Magi
Presentation in the Temple

The Paintings in the Pinacoteca Vaticana

The Paintings in the Pinacoteca Vaticana

on the preceding pages:

Raphael
Transfiguration (1520)

Vatican Museums, Pinacoteca

and details
Raphael, Giulio Romano and Giovan Francesco Penni
The Apostles and the Boy Possessed by Evil

When Raphael died (1520) he had not yet finished the *Transfiguration*; the scene
at the bottom was completed by Giulio Romano and Giovan Francesco Penni. At the top
is the scene on Mount Tabor: Jesus, between Elijah and Moses, is transfigured before
the disciples. In the bottom part, the apostles are dealing with a boy possessed by evil.
Although Cardinal Giulio de' Medici, later Pope Clement VII, commissioned the *Transfiguration*
in 1515 for the cathedral in Narbonne, it was placed in San Pietro in Montorio in Rome.
It was taken to France by Napoleon's troops and was returned to the Vatican in 1816.

Michelangelo and Raphael in the Vatican

Michelangelo and Raphael in the Vatican

Raphael
The Theological Virtues:
Hope, Faith and *Charity* (1507),
predella panels from the *Baglioni Altarpiece*
Vatican Museums, Pinacoteca

The monochrome predella with the three
theological Virtues flanked by winged *putti*,
was destined for the altarpiece
commissioned by Atalanta Baglioni
for the chapel of San Francesco al Prato
in Perugia.

Essential Bibliography

Michelangelo

C. Acidini Luchinat, *Michelangelo scultore*, Milan 2006.

C. Acidini Luchinat, *Michelangelo pittore*, Milan 2007.

R. Di Stefano, *La cupola di San Pietro. Storia della costruzione e dei restauri*, Naples 1980.

F. Hartt, *Michelangelo's Three Pietà*, New York 1975.

M. Hirst, *Michelangelo. The Achievement of Fame*, New Haven-London 2010.

A. Paolucci, *Michelangelo. Le Pietà*, Milan 1997.

H. W. Pfeiffer, *La Sistina svelata. Iconografia di un capolavoro*, Milan-Rome 2007, 2010.

Prefettura della Casa Pontificia, *La Cappella Paolina*, Vatican City 2009.

R. Wittkower, *La cupola di San Pietro di Michelangelo*, Florence 1964.

Raphael

D. Redig de Campos, *Le Stanze di Raffaello*, Florence 1950.

J. Shearman, "The Vatican Stanze: Function and Decoration", in *Proceedings of the British Academy*, 57, London 1971.

Raffaello in Vaticano, exhibition catalogue (Vatican City, Braccio di Carlo Magno, 16 October 1984 - 16 January 1985), ed. by F. Mancinelli and A. M. De Strobel, Rome 1984-1985.

A. Nesselrath, *Raphael's School of Athens*, Vatican City 1996.

N. Dacos, *Le Logge di Raffaello. L'antico, la Bibbia, la bottega, la fortuna*, Milan 2008.

Raphael Cartoons and Tapestries for the Sistine Chapel, exhibition catalogue (London, Victoria and Albert Museum, 8 September - 17 October 2010), ed. by M. Evans and A. Maria De Strobel, London 2010.

Raphaël, les dernières années, exhibition catalogue (Paris, Musée du Louvre, 11 October 2012 - 13 January 2013), ed. by T. Henry and P. Joannides, Paris 2012.

[Translator's notes]

[1] Giorgio Vasari, *Lives of the Painters Sculptors and Architects*, Vol. II, p. 652; trans. by Gaston du C. de Vere, © 1996 by David Campbell Publishers Ltd.

[2] Dante Alighieri, *Divine Comedy*, trans. Charles Eliot Norton, University of Chicago ©1952.

[3] http://www.gutenberg.org/catalog/world/ readfile?fk_files=1476303&pageno=15

[4] Tr. note: in Italian *Rovere* means oak.

[5] Vasari 1996, *op. cit.*, Vol. II, p. 714.

[6] *Ibidem*, p. 717.

[7] http://www.mcah.columbia.edu/ arthumanities/pdfs/arthum_michel_reader.pdf

[8] Vasari 1996, *op. cit.*, Preface to the Third Part, Vol. I, p. 620.

[9] *Ibidem*, p. 746.